NEW ZEALAND

GRAEME LAY

★★★ Highly recommended
★★ Recommended
★ See if you can

This edition is published by Connaught
an imprint of New Holland Publishers Ltd
London • Cape Town • Sydney • Auckland
First published in MM

10 9 8 7 6 5 4 3 2 1
website: www.newhollandpublishers.com

Garfield House,
86 Edgware Road,
London W2 2EA,
United Kingdom

80 McKenzie Street,
Cape Town 8001,
South Africa

14 Aquatic Drive,
Frenchs Forest,
NSW 2086,
Australia

218 Lake Road, Northcote,
Auckland, New Zealand

ISBN 978 1 84517 169 8

Publishing Manager: Thea Grobbelaar
DTP Cartographic Manager: Genené Hart
Editors: Melany McCallum, Thea Grobbelaar
Cartographers: Genené Hart, Marisa Roman
Consultant: Jill Malcolm

Design and DTP: Nicole Bannister, Éloïse Moss
Picture Researchers: Shavonne Govender, Carmen Watts, Sonya Meyer

Reproduction by Hirt & Carter (Pty) Ltd, Cape Town
Printed and bound by Times Offset (M) Sdn. Bhd., Malaysia.

Acknowledgements:
The author would like to thank Christchurch & Canterbury Marketing, Dunedin Tourist Promotion Association, Destination Queenstown, and Qantas New Zealand (formerly Ansett New Zealand), for their co-operation and valuable assistance.

Photographic Credits:
Christchurch & Canterbury Marketing: page 86; **Gerald Cubitt:** pages 9, 10, 12, 13, 25, 36, 39, 40, 41, 42, 43, 49, 50, 52, 56, 59, 61, 76, 77, 90, 100, 116, 118, 119; **Andrew Fear Photography:** cover; **Michael Kelly:** page 97; **Graeme Lay:** page 22; **Life File/Paul Miles:** page 37; **PhotoBank/Adrian Baker:** page 4; **PhotoBank/Gordon Smith:** page 104; **Neil Setchfield:** cover (top right), title page, pages 8, 18, 19, 20, 30, 32, 34, 35, 46, 64, 67, 74, 82; **Jeroen Snijders:** cover (top left, bottom left and right), 6, 7, 11, 14, 15, 16, 17 [left and right], 21, 23, 24, 26, 27, 28, 29, 51, 53, 54, 55, 57, 58, 66, 69, 72, 75, 79, 85, 93, 94, 95, 96, 102, 103, 105, 108, 110, 111, 112, 113, 114, 115, 117.

Keep us Current
Information in travel guides is apt to change, which is why we regularly update our guides. We'd be grateful to receive feedback if you've noted something we should include in our updates. If you have new information, please share it with us by writing to the Publishing Manager, Globetrotter, at the office nearest to you (addresses on this page). The most significant contribution to each new edition will receive a free copy of the updated guide.

Cover Photographs:
Top left: *Akaroa Harbour and its settlement on Banks Peninsula.*
Top right: *The City Loop tram in Christchurch.*
Bottom left: *The Octagon in central Dunedin.*
Bottom right: *Te Mata Peak, with a view of the Hawke's Bay area*

Title Page: *Chaffers Marina, Oriental Bay, Wellington.*

CONTENTS

1 Introducing New Zealand

New Zealand is an **elongated land** extending through 13° of latitude. With two large islands and several smaller ones, the land area totals 265,150km² (164,393 sq miles). The islands are isolated – the nearest large neighbour, Australia, is over 2000km (1240 miles) away – and were among the very last on Earth to be discovered and settled by human beings, just a thousand years ago.

The islands of New Zealand contain a remarkable **variety of landscapes**. In the far north there are gigantic sand dunes, in the far south a region of sheer-sided fiords. The South Island has a wide spine of snow-covered alps, the Northland coast is filigreed with bays and islands. The central plateau of the North Island is a region of volcanic activity, the eastern part of the South Island includes extensive alluvial plains. The islands' landscapes include forested mountains, glaciers, live volcanoes, deep sounds, alpine lakes, gulf islands, and even a cold desert.

The slender shape of both main islands means that nowhere in New Zealand is far from the **sea**. The country's coastline is exceptionally long and varied. An important consequence of this is that nearly all New Zealanders grow up within easy reach of the sea and have an abiding love of it. Boating, fishing, swimming and surfing are treasured aspects of the people's heritage and can also be relished by visitors from abroad. The small amount of heavy industry and the land's exposure to strong winds means that **skies** are unusually **clear and bright** at most times of the year. New Zealanders are justifiably proud of their country's 'clean, green' image, and work hard to maintain it.

Top Attractions

*** **Bay of Islands:** a complex of sheltered islands, bays and beaches.
*** **Rotorua:** hot water lakes, geysers, mud pools, dormant volcanoes and thermal springs.
*** **Tongariro Crossing:** a walk across a volcanic cone and crater, around an active volcano and emerald lakes.
*** **Abel Tasman National Park:** mountains, native forest and birds, right alongside a series of deserted bays and golden sand beaches.
*** **Queenstown:** an alpine town, the adventure capital of New Zealand.

Opposite: *Carved Maori portal, Whakarewarewa Thermal Reserve, Rotorua.*

Facts and Figures

- **Highest point:** Aoraki Mount Cook – 3,754m (12313ft)
- **Lowest point:** The bottom of Lake Hauroko (Fiordland) – 306m (1004ft) below sea level
- **Largest lake:** Taupo – 606km² (376 sq miles)
- **Deepest lake:** Hauroko – 462m (1515ft)
- **River with strongest flow:** Clutha – 650m³ (22,248ft³) per second
- **Largest glacier:** Tasman – 29km (18 miles) long
- **Deepest cave:** Nettlebed, Mount Arthur – 889m (2916ft)
- **Town furthest from the sea:** Cromwell – 120km (74.5 miles)
- **Length of the New Zealand coastline:** 5650km (3503 miles)

New Zealand is a large country in relation to its population size. The total land area is not much less than that of Italy, Japan or Britain, yet New Zealand's population of 4,075,000 is infinitesimal compared with the number of people who live in those countries. Apart from urban congestion on the Auckland isthmus, New Zealand is uncrowded. In much of the North Island and most of the South, coasts, roads and inland areas seem 'empty' to overseas visitors, so that touring by road is delightful. Two-thirds of the population live in the North Island.

Today, the New Zealand population is a mixture of Europeans and Polynesians. The indigenous people, the **Maori**, are descendants of the first immigrants who arrived a millennium ago; most Pakeha (of European descent) are descendants of immigrants who escaped from the poverty of 19th-century Britain.

Recent immigration from south and east Asia and eastern Europe has added other exotic elements to urban populations. Thus, all New Zealanders could be described as **immigrants**. They are noted for their informality, friendliness and lack of class consciousness. Egalitarianism is a valued precept, and tolerance of differences has become more pronounced as New Zealanders have travelled more widely in recent years and experienced other cultures.

For the visitor from overseas, New Zealand offers a wide diversity of both physical and cultural appeal. A country unspoiled by industrial excess or overpopulation, it is a land that was made for physical adventure, and few other places in the world are as geared as New Zealand to participating in its environment in every imaginable way. After all, this is the nation that gave the world, among other things, bungy jumping.

Below: *A view looking south across Lake Taupo, with Mount Tongariro in the background.*

THE LAND

Geologically, New Zealand is a **new and fractured land**, relatively recently raised from beneath the sea. Most of the surface rock is less than 100 million years old and the land is still being actively shaped by earth-building forces. This is because the islands lie close to where two of the world's greatest tectonic plates come into contact.

Above: *The roof of New Zealand: Mount Tasman (the left of the two highest peaks) and Aoraki Mount Cook (right) crown the South Island's beautiful Southern Alps.*

Just east of the North Island the Pacific Plate 'collides' with the Indo-Australian Plate. As the latter is drawn under the Pacific Plate, the crust is heated, then rises as magma in the **Taupo Volcanic Zone**, in the central North Island. This is a region of intense and dramatically active volcanism. In the south of New Zealand the collision of the two plates buckled the crust, thrusting it up to form the **Southern Alps**. An enormous fault line – the **Alpine Fault** – extends diagonally for almost the entire length of the South Island, from Milford Sound to Cook Strait, creating a zone of instability where earthquakes are common.

The **Southern Alps** are New Zealand's most spectacular landform, a broad sierra of snow-covered peaks, glacial lakes and valleys, braided rivers, giant glaciers and intermontane basins. New Zealand's highest peak,

A LAND LIFTED HIGH

Over two-thirds of New Zealand slopes at greater than 12°, and nearly half of the land at greater than 28°. Three-fifths of New Zealand is over 300m (984ft) in altitude, and one-fifth is over 900m (2952ft). Half of the land is farmed, with another 30% being forested. Even the highest and most barren areas are used, mainly for mountain climbing, tramping and skiing.

Aoraki Mount Cook at 3754m (12,313ft), stands amid these alps. There are majestic **fiords** in the extreme southwest of the South Island, and a lovely maze of islands and peninsulas – the **Marlborough Sounds** – at the opposite extreme. In the east are the **Canterbury Plains**, New Zealand's largest lowland. A deep, storm-tossed channel, **Cook Strait**, separates the two main islands.

The **North Island**'s topography is more diverse. A spine of heavily dissected mountains averaging 1500m (4,920ft) extends to the northeast, flanked by fertile lowlands. In the centre of the island is the **Volcanic Plateau**, Lake Taupo and a high, cold desert region. The North Island's highest mountain, the active volcano Mount Ruapehu, 2797m (9,174ft), is located here.

The North Island tapers away in a northwesterly direction, becoming a region of **peninsulas**, deep **bays**, indented **harbours** and **islands**. Here the sea – the Tasman to the west, the Pacific Ocean to the east – is almost always in sight. New Zealand's northern extremity is **Cape Reinga**, a place of deep spiritual significance to the Maori people and the turbulent meeting point of these two seas.

There is a marked **difference** between the **west and east coasts** of both islands. In the west, strong prevailing winds create boisterous swells and strong waves, very suitable for surfing. On the relatively sheltered eastern coasts the sea is more subdued. Here the white sand beaches, tranquil bays and tidal inlets are ideal for swimming, fishing, boating and diving. There are also many excellent surfing areas on the east coast. There are sharks present along both coasts, particularly in summer, but shark attacks are extremely rare in New Zealand.

The Shaky Isles

New Zealand is noted for the frequency of its **earthquakes**. On average there are 17,000 each year, most of which are too deep-seated to be felt by anything other than a seismograph. Six of these, however, are greater than magnitude 6 on the Richter Scale, meaning they are big enough to cause major destruction if they occur near the surface and strike a town or city.

The **Wellington Fault** runs right through the centre of the capital city, and Wellingtonians are used to feeling the earth move beneath their feet. In 1855, when it was just a town of 6000 people, a massive earthquake raised the coast to the east of Wellington by a staggering 6m (20ft). Today, such a 'quake would cause untold devastation, in spite of the fact that the city's high-rise buildings were 'earthquake-proofed' during the 1970s and 1980s.

Climate

New Zealand's climate can be classified as **maritime** and **temperate**, which is the result of three factors: its ocean setting, its location in the path of prevailing westerly winds, and the mountain backbone of both the main islands. The mountains serve to modify the strength of the winds, and they also provide a sheltering effect on their leeward side. Therefore, the major **contrast** in New Zealand's climate is between the **western** and the **eastern** parts of the country, with the west coast being much wetter than the east.

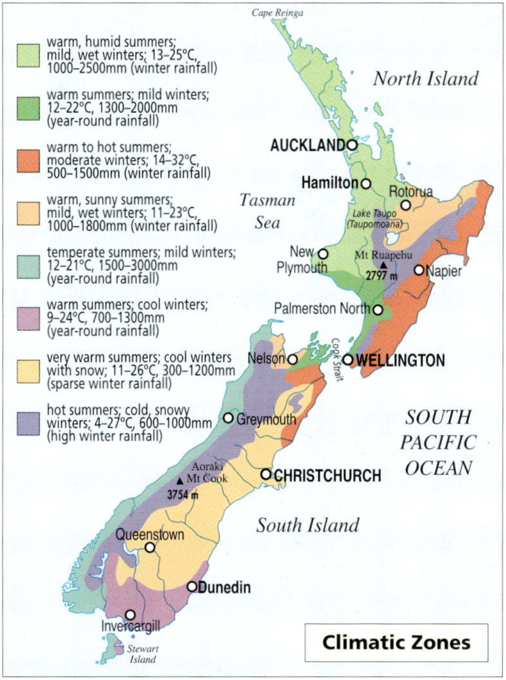

Opposite: *Pohutu Geyser, one of the main attractions in the Whakarewarewa Thermal Reserve, Rotorua, is an impressive sight when it spouts steam.*
Left: *This beach, typical of Northland's coastline, is located in Araiteuru Reserve, near Omapere.*

CLIMATIC EXTREMES

- Highest North Island temperature: 39.2°C (104°F), Ruatoria, East Coast, 7 February 1973.
- Highest South Island temperature: 42.4°C (108°F), Rangiora, North Canterbury, 7 February 1973.
- Lowest North Island temperature: -13.6°C (-57°F), Chateau Tongariro, Mount Ruapehu, 7 July, 1937.
- Lowest South Island temperature: - 21.6°C (-71°F), Ophir, Central Otago, 3 July 1995.
- Highest North Island annual sunshine hours: Napier, 2588 hours, 1994.
- Highest South Island annual sunshine hours: Nelson, 2711 hours, 1931.
- Highest 12-month rainfall total: Waterfall Creek, Westland, 1982-83, 14,108mm (550 in).
- Strongest wind gust: 250 km/h, Mount John, Canterbury, 18 April 1970.

The weather (the day-to-day temperatures as well as the rainfall) is produced by a series of **alternating high and low pressure systems** which move across New Zealand from the Tasman Sea, bringing with them changeable conditions. Typically, there will be about 2–3 days of settled weather, followed by a similar period of unsettled conditions.

There are **few extremes** of climate, with mild temperatures and moderate rainfall being the normal pattern in most areas, although winds coming from the southerly quarter bring snowfalls to upland areas of both islands from June through to September. Only Central Otago (the South Island region furthest from the sea and surrounded by mountains) experiences the very cold, dry winters and hot dry summers of a continental-type climate.

Rainfall is particularly heavy in the southwest and west of the South Island, where the high mountains force up the rain-bearing westerlies, which then release their moisture on the windward slopes of the mountains. In this part of the country the annual rainfall averages over 12,800mm (499in).

Opposite: *These impressive giant kauri trees are to be found in the Waipoua Forest, Northland.*
Right: *The Whakapapa ski-field at Mount Ruapehu in Tongariro National Park is very popular with visitors, especially at the height of the season.*

The weather in New Zealand is most settled from February through to April, when temperatures are generally warm to hot and rainfall is low. For those who enjoy tramping, swimming or boating, this is the best time to visit New Zealand. The winter sports season in the South Island usually begins in June and ends in October, and on the North Island ski-fields around Mount Ruapehu, winter begins in July and lasts right through September.

Flora and Fauna

New Zealand's natural vegetation was **forest**, a consequence of its moist, temperate climate. There are two types of native forest – coniferous podocarps and southern beech – both types evergreen, which in pre-European times covered about half the total land area.

The 19th- and early 20th-century settlers **cleared the forests** ruthlessly, replacing them with pasture, so that today only 30% of the land is forested. Nevertheless, the remaining areas of native forest, with their unique tree species, are places of great beauty and tranquillity. Trees such as kauri, rimu, totara, miro, kahikatea, matai, rata in the North Island, and the beech forests of

The Mighty Kauri

A native of New Zealand, the majestic kauri (*Agathis australis*) is a giant conifer which grows naturally only north of 38° latitude. It has a rounded 'stag-headed' crown supported by a huge cylindrical trunk up to 7m (23ft) in diameter and can attain a height of 60m (197ft). Ravaged by millers until the early 20th century for its timber, the remaining examples are strictly protected and can be seen in the Waipoua and Trounson forests in western Northland, and in parts of Coromandel, where there are some magnificent specimens. They can live to 2000 years. The Kauri Museum at Matakohe, 45km (28 miles) south of Dargaville, has extensive displays illustrating the historical significance of the kauri to the Northland economy.

A National Emblem Threatened

The flightless kiwi is New Zealand's emblem and New Zealanders themselves are often known affectionately as 'kiwis'. Ironically as well as sadly, the national bird is today a highly endangered species. There are three species of kiwi: the brown (*Apteryx australis*), the great spotted (*A. haastii*) and the little spotted (*A. owenii*). Kiwis are nocturnal, foraging on the forest floor with their long beaks for insects and other invertebrates. Dogs, stoats, ferrets and rats prey on the kiwi and its eggs, so that over 95% of kiwi chicks die in the wild. Thus, the bird's main chance of long-term survival lies with the populations living in zoos and on New Zealand's predator-free off-shore islands.

the South Island are today **protected** and valued for their recreational value. Many species of tree ferns, such as the ponga, occupy the forest floors and damp gullies, and the nikau is a particularly handsome palm which grows in both islands.

When New Zealand 'drifted' away from the ancient continent of Gondwana about 80 million years ago to its **isolated position** in the Southwest Pacific, land-distributed plants and animal immigrants were unable to reach the land. Winged immigrants were able to settle, however, and many did so, coming mainly from Australia. Many birds which reached New Zealand in ancient times subsequently became flightless, due to the lack of natural predators. The moa, long extinct, and the kiwi, takahe and kakapo – today all highly endangered species – are the best-known examples.

Some surviving representatives of Gondwana fauna are the **tuatara**, member of a very early order of reptiles, and the **native frog**. On the forest floor earthworms, wetas (large flightless insects belonging to the cricket family), centipedes, spiders and large carnivorous snails are animals inherited from Gondwana times. The only

native land mammals are two **bat** species – the short-tailed and the long-tailed bat – but there are several native species of skink and gecko which, unusually, give birth to live young.

New Zealand's forests were rich in **bird life** long before the arrival of human beings, approximately 1000 years ago. Species such as the tui, bellbird, huia, native pigeon, morepork, saddleback, kokako, the kea and the kaka found an ideal home in the forest habitats of both islands.

Humans introduced **predators**, however, which decimated the native bird population. The Maori hunted all species of moa to extinction within 500 years of their arrival, and introduced dogs and the kiore (the Polynesian rat) which attacked the young of the flightless birds. European settlers introduced cats, dogs, rats, stoats, ferrets and opossums, all of which prey on the vulnerable eggs, chicks and mature birds. Widespread clearance of the birds' natural habitat, the native forests, has also contributed to their threatened status. The huia became extinct about 100 years ago, while today the takahe, kokako, kakapo and kiwi hover on the brink of extinction.

To help stave off this extinction, many **off-shore islands** are **wildlife reserves** free of all introduced mammals. The most important of these sanctuaries are: Little Barrier, Kapiti, Maud and Codfish Islands.

New Zealand's Ancient Reptile

The tuatara (*Sphenodon punctatus*) is a unique archaic animal which survives only in zoos and on New Zealand's off-shore islands. It belongs to a very early order of reptiles, the Sphenodontida, which appeared at the time that the dinosaurs were evolving, about 230 million years ago. The tuatara are now the only surviving Sphenodontida. They are amphibious, and reproduce by means of the male and female pressing their genital openings together so that sperm passes from the male to the female. Rat-free Stephens Island, north of the Marlborough Sounds, is home to New Zealand's largest tuatara population.

Opposite: *The great spotted kiwi is a nocturnal-foraging bird.*
Below: *A tuatara on Little Barrier Island, a wildlife sanctuary near Auckland.*

VIEWING ENDANGERED SPECIES

New Zealand's endangered national bird, the kiwi, along with other native birds and tuatara, can be seen at the Kiwi House Native Bird Park in the small King Country town of Otorohanga, about 50km (31 miles) south of Hamilton. Mount Bruce National Wildlife Centre in the northern Wairarapa is a vital centre for captive-breeding of kiwi, takahe, kokako, saddleback and kakapo. Here the birds live in large aviaries among a pre-served stand of native forest.

HISTORY IN BRIEF

The first arrivals in New Zealand came from **eastern Polynesia**, the islands today called French Polynesia and the Cook Islands, approximately 1000 years ago. They sailed in double-hulled, catamaran-like canoes and navigated by the stars to cross the several thousand kilometres of open ocean between their islands and the new land. Return voyages to the islands of tropical Polynesia almost certainly occurred. The generic name for these people is **Maori**.

The islands these Polynesians called **Aotearoa** ('Land of the Long White Cloud') were much cooler and larger than the tropical islands they had left behind, but after a few hundred years they had **adapted skilfully** to their **new environment**, hunting and trapping birds, cultivating the kumara (sweet potato), catching fish, hunting seals and fashioning tools from stone and greenstone. They lived tribally in villages and fortified hill settlements called pa.

Opposite: *An ornately carved Maori storehouse, or pataka, in Waiotapu.*
Below: *A Maori war canoe, also called a waka, at Waitangi, Bay of Islands.*

European Contact

The first European sailing expedition to sight New Zealand was that commanded by the Dutch explorer,

Abel Tasman, in 1642. A fatal skirmish with Maori in the northwest of the South Island drove the expedition away, however, and Tasman charted only part of the New Zealand coastline. Vastly more far-reaching and influential was the expedition of **Captain James Cook**, which entered the South Pacific in 1769 in search of the mythical continent, called *Terra incognita australis*, and also to observe the transit of the planets Venus and Mercury.

Historical Calendar

c1000 Approximate arrival of first Polynesian immigrants.
c1300 Polynesian settlement established in both islands.
1642 Abel Tasman charts part of the coast and calls it Staten Land. Another Dutchman later changes it to Nieuw Zeeland.
1769 James Cook makes first visit, taking the land in the name of King George III.
1814 First Anglican mission station established. Sheep, cattle and horses introduced.
1821 Inter-tribal Maori musket wars. Widespread slaughter.
1839 Captain William Hobson instructed to establish British rule in New Zealand.
1840 New Zealand Company settlers arrive in Wellington. Treaty of Waitangi signed at Bay of Islands. British sovereignty; Auckland seat of government.
1865 The capital is transferred to Wellington.
1877 The Education Act establishes a national system of primary education.
1886 Mt Tarawera erupts, destroying Pink and White Terraces and killing 153 people.
1893 Franchise is extended to women.
1907 New Zealand is constituted as a Dominion.
1914 German Samoa occupied by New Zealand Forces. Expeditionary Forces sent to Egypt.
1935 First Labour Government elected under Michael Savage.
1939 Second New Zealand Expeditionary Force formed.
1953 First tour of New Zealand by a reigning English monarch. Edmund Hillary and Tenzing Norgay conquer Mt Everest.
1960 Regular television programmes begin in Auckland.
1966 International airport officially opens at Auckland.
1968 Inter-island ferry *Wahine* sinks in a storm in Wellington Harbour, 51 people die.
1973 Britain becomes member of EEC, necessitating new markets for New Zealand exports.
1979 Air New Zealand DC 10 crashes on Mt Erebus, Antarctica, killing 257 people.
1984 Labour Party wins snap election; Finance Minister Roger Douglas begins deregulating the economy.
1995 Team New Zealand wins the America's Cup.
1999 APEC conference held in Auckland.
2000 New Zealand successfully defends the America's Cup against Prada of Italy.
1999 New Zealand's first elected woman prime minister, Helen Clark, becomes country's leader.
2001 New Zealand-made film, *The Fellowship of the Ring*, the first of the *Lord of the Rings* trilogy, is released worldwide.
2003 Population reaches 4m. New Zealand loses America's Cup to Swiss syndicate, Alinghi.
2004 Third film in *Lord of the Rings* trilogy, *The Return of the King*, wins 11 Oscar awards.

Above: *A bust and a portrait of Captain Cook at Te Papa (National Museum of New Zealand), Wellington.* **Opposite left:** *The Maori war dance, or haka, at Waitangi, Bay of Islands.* **Opposite right:** *The original of the Treaty of Waitangi, signed on 6 February 1840.*

Cook circumnavigated the islands of New Zealand, charted their waters brilliantly and made significant contacts with the Maori. He estimated that there were about 100,000 Maori living throughout the islands. Upon Cook's return to Britain, publication of his journals aroused great **interest in the South Pacific**, and from the 1790s onwards a succession of Europeans set sail for New Zealand, with many and varied motives. Traders, sealers, whalers, missionaries and adventurers came to the islands, bringing with them European goods, the gospels and infectious diseases.

A Colony of Britain

New Zealand did not officially become a British colony, however, until 1840, when the **Treaty of Waitangi** was signed in the Bay of Islands between the Crown and a number of Maori chiefs. This ceded New Zealand to Britain while theoretically protecting Maori land and fishing rights. British rule, however, led to an influx of European settlement over the next decades, culminating in **mass immigration** during the 1860s and 1870s. Disputes between Maori and Europeans over land sales and settlement led to war between the two during the 1860s. Wars – both inter-tribal and with European authorities – and introduced diseases caused a drastic decline in the Maori population.

The discovery of **gold** in the 1860s gave further impetus to European immigration. Between 1861 and 1891 net immigration to New Zealand was 272,990 – the main sources of migrants being England, Scotland, Ireland, Wales and Australia. These settlers sought land of their own, and **cleared the native bush** ruthlessly, particularly

Annual Holidays

New Year (1 and 2 January)
Waitangi Day (6 February)
Good Friday
Easter Monday
Anzac Day (25 April)
Queen's Birthday (first Monday in June)
Labour Day (last Monday in October)
Christmas Day (25 December)
Boxing Day (26 December)

in the North Island, to convert it to **pastureland** for cattle and sheep. The advent of refrigerated shipping in 1882 led to substantial exports of frozen meat, butter and cheese, almost all of which was sent to Britain.

The 20th Century

New Zealand's 20th century history was dominated by the **two world wars**, in both of which the young nation was a fervent supporter of the British cause, and alternating periods of economic boom and depression.

The slaughter of New Zealand and Australian troops by Turkish forces during the Gallipoli campaign in April 1915 gave rise to **Anzac Day**, a national holiday celebrated every year on 25 April, when all the country's war casualties are commemorated. Some 16,781 New Zealanders died in World War I, a huge number considering that the nation's total population only reached one million in 1908. During World War II New Zealand forces **served the Allied cause** against Germany in North Africa, the Mediterranean and Italy, and against Japan in the Pacific. Again, casualties were high.

In the years following World War II, New Zealand prospered. The Korean War of the early 1950s (to which New Zealand contributed ground and naval forces) also caused **a boom in wool prices**. Assisted immigration from Britain and the Netherlands brought more new settlers.

Ozone Loss

Ozone is a stratospheric gas which provides protection for humans from destructive ultra-violet radiation. The amount of ultra-violet radiation in New Zealand has increased by approximately 15% over the last 30 years as a result of ozone depletion. This is caused by the release of chlorofluorocarbon molecules – used as coolants in refrigerators and propellants in spray cans – into the atmosphere. The result is that a significant ozone 'hole' has developed over Antarctica in recent years, and during the Antarctic spring (October to December) up to 60% of the ozone layer disappears, increasing the intensity of the sun's rays. Human skin thus burns very quickly during the New Zealand summer, and sun block must be applied and sun hats worn, particularly by those who have a fair skin, to prevent skin cancer.

THE VILLA

The most distinctive New Zealand residential building is the bay villa, examples of which are found in the cities' older suburbs. The bay villa was most popular from 1895-1910. Usually built of kauri, villas have weatherboard walls, a front verandah and bay, large sash windows, shingled gables topped with finials, and a corrugated iron roof. The verandah is embellished with fretworked brackets and spindles. The elegance, spaciousness and relative rarity of the villas have led to a renewed appreciation of them in recent years, and many are now being renovated and restored to their Victorian glory.

Inflation and unemployment were negligible. The population reached two million in 1952, and trade boosted the growth of city ports like Auckland, Wellington and Christchurch. Work opportunities in towns and cities, and the increased mechanization of farming, led to a **migration** of people from **rural areas** into the growing **urban centres**. Maori were particularly affected as they moved from their traditional rural tribal districts to the cities to take up largely unskilled work in factories and food processing plants.

Strategically, New Zealand perceived a threat to its security from communist 'expansion' in south and east Asia. Troops were sent to Malaya in 1956 to help counter insurgency, to Malaysia in 1962 during that country's 'confrontation' with Indonesia, and to Vietnam from 1965 until 1971 to assist the United States' cause.

The demand for factory labour continued in the 1970s, and a new source of **immigrants**, the **islands of the South Pacific**, was tapped. People from Western Samoa, Tonga, Niue Island, the Tokelaus and the Cook Islands, all of which New Zealand had had close political affiliations with during the early 20th century, migrated to Auckland and Wellington, driven from their home islands by a lack of work and low wages. In 1961 there were 14,300 Pacific Islanders in New Zealand. By 1971 there were 43,700, by 1981 nearly 94,000, by 1996 nearly 217,000, and by 2002 the Pacific Island population was approaching a quarter of a million, or 6.5% of the total population.

In 1973 Britain became a member of the EEC and oil prices were substantially 'hiked', necessitating **changes** in New Zealand's **economic direction**. Trade became more diversified, with closer ties to Australia, Japan and North America, and domestic sources of natural gas and oil developed.

Above left: *Queen Street is Auckland city's main commercial thoroughfare.* **Opposite:** *This attractively painted Victorian-era wooden house at Oriental Bay, Wellington, incorporates several characteristics of the villa, including sash and bay windows.*

The election of the Fourth Labour Government in 1984 brought a radical **restructuring** of the economy. The dollar was devalued by 20%, subsidies were eliminated and all controls on foreign exchange transactions and overseas borrowing were removed. Many formerly protected industries collapsed, causing a sharp increase in unemployment. In 1986 a 10% Goods and Services Tax (GST) was introduced, and it was raised to 12.5% in 1989. The Labour Government was re-elected in 1987, but share prices plummeted by 59% during four months of the same year, leading to recession and the election of a National Government in 1990.

The 1990s were characterized by **slow economic growth**, high unemployment and a significant increase in immigration from Asian countries such as Taiwan, South Korea, Hong Kong, Japan, China and India, and from South Africa, the Middle East and Eastern Europe. From 1991–96 there were nearly 89,000 immigrant arrivals from Asia. Consequently New Zealand's population has become increasingly **multicultural** and polyglot, with strands of the South Pacific, Asia and the Middle East readily apparent in the major cities. Ethnic restaurants and street markets have proliferated, adding to the cities' cosmopolitan atmosphere. The rural areas have been largely unaffected by these trends, however, and in the many small country towns the subdued pace and homogeneity of life continues much as before.

Living in the City

Today two-thirds of New Zealanders live in centres with more than 30,000 people. Auckland is dominant: over a quarter of the total population lives there. During the last 50 years, as well as substantial rural-urban migration, there has been a 'Northward Drift' of population and, in recent years, the South Island has had a small net gain of people. Today there are over three million people in the North Island and nearly one million in the South Island.

Above: *The 'Beehive' (left) and Parliament House, central Wellington.*
Below: *The New Zealand flag incorporates the Union Jack and Southern Cross.*

GOVERNMENT AND ECONOMY

New Zealand is an independent state, a **monarchy with a parliamentary government**. Queen Elizabeth II has the title 'Queen of New Zealand'. The Governor-General is the representative of the Sovereign in New Zealand and exercises the royal powers derived from statute and the general law. The Governor-General's main constitutional function is to arrange for the leader of the majority party in Parliament to form a government. The Governor-General's assent is also required before bills can become law, though the Governor-General is required to follow the advice of the ministers of the Crown. The Sovereign appoints the Governor-General on the recommendation of the Prime Minister, for a 5-year term. From 1840–1967 Governors-General were chosen from British nobility. **Sir Arthur Porritt** GCMG, GCVO, CBE (b Wanganui, 1900), who was Governor-General from 1967–72, was the **first New Zealand-born** holder of the post, and subsequent Governors-General have been New Zealanders. **Dame Catherine Tizard** GCMG, GCVO, DBE, QSO, who held the post from 1990–95, was the **first woman** Governor-General. The current Governor-General is also a woman, **Dame Silvia Cartwright** PCNZM, DBE.

New Zealand's **Constitution Act 1996** brings together the most important statutory constitutional provisions and clarifies the rules relating to the governmental hand-over of power, dealing with the roles of the Sovereign, the Executive, the legislature and the judiciary. Although the constitution is theoretically a monarchy, it operates democratically through New Zealand's long tradition of parliamentary government. The Government cannot act effectively without Parliament, as it cannot raise or spend money without parliamentary approval.

The Flag

The flag is the symbol of the realm, government and people of New Zealand. The flag's design consists of the Union Jack in the upper left quarter, and on a dark blue background to the right, the Southern Cross is represented by four 5-pointed stars with white borders.

Local governments are largely independent of central government, though their powers are conferred by Parliament. They have their own sources of income, primarily **local taxes** on landed property. These taxes, called **rates**, are set by local authorities, based on the value of land and buildings. Local authorities can promote legislation about matters affecting areas in their jurisdiction, and are answerable to the electorates through **general elections**, held every three years, in which all ratepayers are entitled to vote.

A TRADING NATION

The vast majority of New Zealand's exports and imports are moved by sea. In 1996 New Zealand's ports loaded and unloaded 99% of overseas cargo by volume, and over 90% by value. International air freight generally consists of fragile, perishable and expensive items such as cut flowers.

Some New Zealand ports are net exporters, generally reflecting their location close to extractive industries. These ports include Bluff (aluminium smelter), Tauranga (forest products) and Napier (farm produce). Three ports, namely Auckland, Auckland Airport and Whangarei, are net importers, the first two importing to meet consumer demands, and Whangarei being where the country's oil refinery is located.

The Economy

In spite of the radical reforms of the 1980s, New Zealand's **economic growth** was slow during the 1990s. A 7–8% unemployment rate, an excess of imports over exports, balance of payment deficits and a high level of overseas debt and debt servicing characterized the economy. **Low prices** for wool and meat made farming (for many years the mainstay of the economy), marginal or uneconomic. Many local manufacturing industries were forced to close down or move 'off-shore' in the face of cheaper imports of consumer goods.

However, from 2002–5 economic growth has been robust. Corporate profits have risen, the stock market has performed well, commodity prices have increased, inflation is low, unemployment at 3.8% is at its lowest level in many years and government accounts have shown healthy surpluses. There has been impressive growth in **tourism** and in **exports** of processed milk products, fruit, flowers, seafood and wine. In the year to September 2004 there were 2,307,470 overseas visitors, a 17% increase in 3 years, and worth over NZ$5 billion to the economy. Tourism and non-traditional exports are replacing traditional, unprocessed primary products like wool and meat, and underscore the need for New Zealand to concentrate on exports of processed products with high added value. Key economic elements for the future will involve obtaining more skilled immigrants and training New Zealanders in the skills necessary for a thoroughly modern, internationally competitive economy.

Below: *The container wharf in Napier handles mainly agricultural exports from the Hawke's Bay area.*

ORDER OF NEW ZEALAND

New Zealand's highest award is the Order of New Zealand (ONZ), which was instituted on 6 February 1987 (Waitangi Day) to recognize outstanding services to the Crown and people of New Zealand in a civil or military capacity. There are no more than 20 ordinary members at any time, and they currently include diva Dame Kiri Te Kanawa, writers Janet Frame and Margaret Mahy, mountaineer Sir Edmund Hillary, architect Sir Miles Warren and industrialist Sir James Fletcher.

The New Zealand Order of Merit is an Order of Chivalry introduced in 1996. The order is for those people who in any field of endeavour have rendered meritorious service to the Crown and nation, or who have become distinguished by their eminence, talents, contributions or other merits. The New Zealand Order of Merit has five levels.

THE PEOPLE

New Zealanders are proud of their **egalitarian tradition**, a result of their forebears' determination to escape the class systems of Britain. Isolation and a pioneer background have also encouraged resourcefulness among New Zealanders, a determined 'do-it-yourself' attitude which means that they are a very practical people. They are also very informal, proud of their achievements in developing a modern, democratic nation in less than 200 years, and welcoming to overseas visitors. A great **love of the outdoors**, sea, coasts, forests and mountains, is matched by a fondness for sharing their pleasures with visitors.

One consequence of their isolation is that New Zealanders are extremely mobile and **well-travelled**, particularly young people, a rite of passage for whom is their 'OE' or Overseas Experience. After travelling the world, the usual pattern is for them to return, although more lucrative working conditions in cities like Sydney, London and New York during the 1990s have tended to prolong their overseas experience. From the beginning of the 21st century, however, more New Zealanders have been returning to live in their homeland.

Although their ways of life were dissimilar, New Zealanders of European descent (Pakeha) and the indigenous people, the Maori, have mostly co-existed easily this century. **Intermarriage** between the two races has been common, so many New Zealanders are of mixed ancestry.

Until the 1970s there were few other races – some Chinese (descendants of 19th-century gold-miners) and some Indians. Racial homogeneity and isolation led to a narrow parochialism among many New Zealanders, but this has changed as internationalism and substantial immigration from the South Pacific and Asia has

diversified the population and led to a much greater tolerance of differences. A number of diverse cultural celebrations such as Pacific and Asian festivals and food and wine festivals are now a regular and eagerly anticipated aspect of the New Zealand social calendar.

The overseas experiences of travelling Kiwis have led to a demand for a **more diverse and sophisticated way of life**, particularly in the field of wining and dining. This demand has been met enthusiastically. Ethnic cafés and restaurants, many with outdoor eating areas, have proliferated since the 1980s, featuring fine New Zealand wines and local ingredients prepared to the recipes of Italy, France, Japan, India, Thailand and Turkey. Unlike the dreary days of the 1950s and 1960s, when it was forbidden to sell alcohol with food, most of these cafés and restaurants are licensed or BYO (bring your own liquor). **Tourism**, both in-bound and out-bound, along with immigration, has brought a new cosmopolitanism to the New Zealand way of life.

Above: *A Maori warrior in traditional costume performing the* haka.
Opposite: *Young Samoan New Zealanders at a cultural festival, Auckland.*

Maori Society

After suffering a serious decline in the mid-19th century, due to introduced infectious diseases, land dispossession and war, Maori **population growth is now vigorous**. In 1996, a total of 523,374 people identified with the Maori ethnic group, an increase of 20.4% on the 1991 figure of 434,844. This means that the Maori ethnic group is now 14.7% of the population, up from 12.9% in 1991. Those who identified Maori as their sole ethnicity totalled 273,693 in 1996. This reflects the trend among New Zealanders to identify with more than one ethnic group.

The regions with the largest Maori populations today are the East Coast, Poverty Bay, Northland and Rotorua. At the other end of the scale, the rural central part of the South Island has less than 5% Maori population.

Intermarriage with Pakeha has always been a feature of Maori society. In 1960, for example, half the marriages contracted by Maori were with Pakeha spouses. Another

The Location of the Maori Population

The timber town of Kawerau, on the Volcanic Plateau, has the highest percentage of Maori people, at 57.94%, and the South Auckland city of Manukau the largest number (42,762).

At the other extreme, the population of the South Island town of Waimate is only 4.02% Maori, while the territorial local authority of Mackenzie in the central South Island has the smallest number of Maori (only 270).

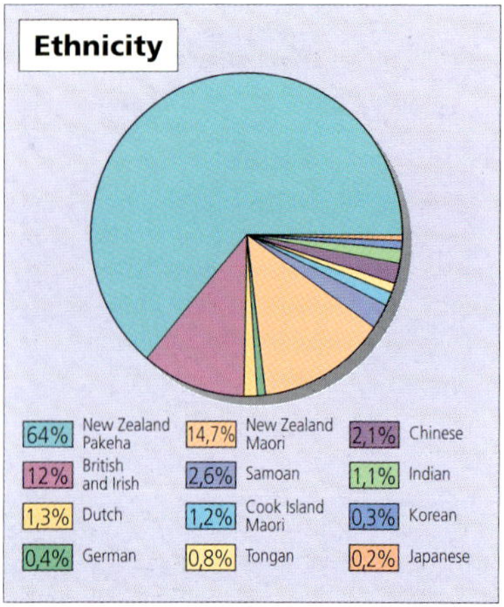

Above right: *A pair of Maori youngsters proudly display their skateboards.*

SOCIAL INDICATORS

Birth Rate: 17:1000
Death Rate: 8:1000
Life Expectancy:
Females – 81 years
Males – 76 years
Fertility rate:
2.04 births per woman
Housing:
70% of New Zealanders own their own home
80% of New Zealanders live in urban areas
Median age:
At the end of 2001 the median age of New Zealanders was 34.7 years
Population growth:
The New Zealand population growth rate is now 1% per year

significant feature of Maori society in the second half of the 20th century was its **rapid urbanization**. From 1950 until the 1980s, 75% of the Maori population migrated from their rural tribal areas to the towns and cities, to which they transplanted adaptations of their culture, such as community activities and *marae*. However, since the rise of unemployment during the 1980s, many urban Maori have returned to their tribal areas, where they have inalienable rights to land and fishing.

By many social criteria, Maori fall behind the population as a whole. In **education**, **health** and particularly **unemployment**, Maori are significantly **disadvantaged**. Between 1986 and 1991 the unemployment rate for Maori increased from 14.9 to 24.2%. The equivalent rates for non-Maori were 5.8 and 9%. Some 38% of Maori leave school without qualifications (13% for non-Maori). Both the birth and death rate are higher for Maori than non-Maori, while life expectancy is lower.

For the first five decades of the 20th century the teaching and speaking of the **Maori language** was discouraged, on the grounds that Maori people would as a result assimilate more rapidly with the Pakeha way of life and thereby progress more rapidly. This policy has changed markedly since the 1960s, however. Since then, the learning of the Maori language has been encouraged, as part of a general **renaissance** in **traditional Maori culture and heritage**. The establishment of Kohanga Reo, Maori language 'nests' for pre-school children, where they are immersed totally in spoken and written Maori, has done much to foster the continuation of the language. In 1997 there were 13,500 children enrolled in Kohanga Reo. The Maori language is now also taught at primary, secondary and tertiary levels of the education system, although a continuing problem is the lack of trained teachers, a sad legacy of the earlier assimilation policy.

Because most of the Maori people now live in the cities, **urban marae** have been established to serve as a focus for community activities. A marae is a place where the tribe, hapu (sub-tribe) or whanau (extended family) see themselves as belonging. The marae consist of a whare runanga, or meeting house, designed in the traditional manner and adorned with woven panels, carved poles and barge boards. Visitors to these city marae are still called onto it by a karanga, given by mature women who belong to it, then greeted according to traditional custom. It is customary for the visitors, or manuhiri, to bring a gift, known as a koha, for the people of the marae. The Greater Auckland area has several such marae, to accommodate the needs of the people from the various tribes who live in the area.

A source of contention has arisen in recent years over whether urban-based Maori, many now second- and third-generation city dwellers, still retain their **customary rights** to valuable commercial fishing resources, most of which are well away from the cities. The New Zealand Court of Appeal has ruled that urban Maori do not retain these rights, a judgement which has caused a division along rural-urban lines.

The Maori electoral population is decided by eligible Maori voters choosing to enrol on either the Maori Roll or the General Roll. There were five Maori electorates for the 1996 General Election and six for the 1999 election. This was based on the Maori descent voter

A PAINTER OF GENIUS

Colin McCahon (1919–87) is considered New Zealand's greatest painter and one who has achieved international acclaim, most of it posthumous. A dark, slim, self-effacing man, he was raised in the South Island and influenced by cubism, modernism and the New Zealand landscape. He moved to Auckland with his wife and children in 1953 and taught at Elam Art School, where he in turn influenced many younger painters. McCahon's paintings were frequently reviled by those who found his abstract style and religious themes baffling, but appreciation of them nevertheless grew, until today they are worth millions of dollars. A chronic alcoholic whose condition was worsened by Korsakov's Syndrome, McCahon died in Auckland Public Hospital in May 1987.

Below: *Pastoral farmland in the Gisborne area, on the North Island's East Coast.*

FRANK SARGESON (1903–82)

Sargeson is considered to be the first fiction writer who truly captured the cadences of New Zealand speech. A short story writer, novelist and playwright, he qualified as a solicitor before devoting his life to writing. He lived in a humble cottage in Takapuna, on Auckland's North Shore, from 1930 until his death. The house, a centre of literary meetings and friendship, is today preserved as a museum by the Sargeson Trust and can be visited by those interested in the writer's life and work. The key is available from the Takapuna Public Library, Takapuna.

option increasing to 628,429 by the 1999 election, with the average population of each electorate the same as for the General electorates, that is 56,166 people. In forming the Maori electorates, the law requires that due consideration be given to community of interest among Maori people generally and also members of tribes, means of communications, topographical features, and any projected variation in the Maori electoral population.

The Arts

Over the last two decades there has been a **burst of artistic activity** in New Zealand which has reflected the maturing of the young nation's national consciousness and a recognition of its position as a South Pacific country with its own **unique national identity**. In art, music, film, drama and literature, New Zealand now has large numbers of accomplished professional practitioners whose work is of international quality.

The breakthrough from colonial to a post-colonial artistic community was made by a number of **visionary individuals**. Painters Rita Angus and Colin McCahon, novelists Jean Devanney and Jane Mander, short story writers Katherine Mansfield and Frank Sargeson, film-maker John O'Shea, architect Vernon Brown, composers Douglas Lilburn and Jenny McLeod, playwright Bruce Mason and poets A.R.D. Fairburn, Ursula Bethell, Allen Curnow and Denis Glover took their art in uniquely New Zealand directions which were further developed by others who followed. As Allen Curnow (1911–2001) wrote in his prophetic 1943 poem, *The Skeleton of the Great Moa in the Canterbury Museum, Christchurch*:

'Not I, some child, born in a marvellous year,
Will learn the trick of standing upright here.'

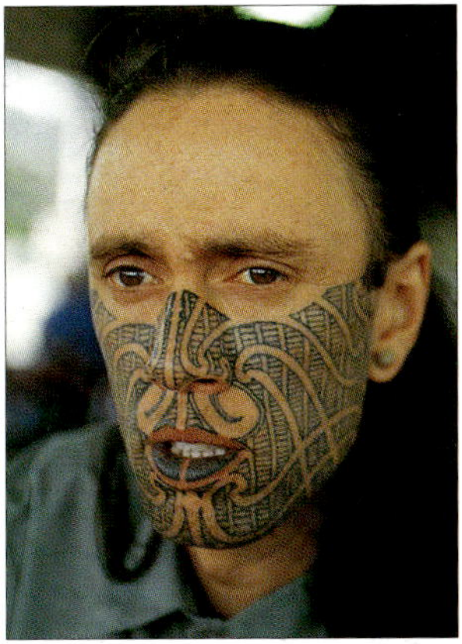

State support for the arts dates back to the 1940 centenary celebrations. The Literary Fund, established in 1946, supported New Zealand writers and publishing. Its work was later continued and broadened to include the performing arts by the Queen Elizabeth II Arts Council, now known as **Creative New Zealand**, the operating name for The Arts Council of New Zealand – Toi Aotearoa. Creative New Zealand receives funding through Vote Cultural Affairs and the New Zealand Lottery Grants Board. A typical Creative New Zealand funding round, announced in October 2004, issued 263 project grants, totalling NZ$3.9 million.

The New Zealand Film Commission was formed in 1978, to help finance a growing number of private film-makers. The most internationally successful New Zealand films supported by the commission have been *Once Were Warriors* and *Whale Rider* (2003). The latter achieved a worldwide box office take of NZ$93.2 million.

The combination of private artistic drive, state support and business sponsorship has seen a proliferation of New Zealand music, painting, film, dance, drama and literature since the 1970s. Overseas film companies have found New Zealand's scenic beauty and technical expertise appealing, and many **films and television series** have been shot here. The largest cinematic project to date is a three-part adaptation of Tolkien's *Lord of the Rings*, the filming of which began in 1999, directed by the internationally acclaimed Wellington-based film-maker, Peter Jackson. The last in the trilogy, *The Return of the King*, was released in 2003.

New Zealand's artistic flowering includes the work of **Maori artists** such as painters Ralph Hotere and Emily Karaka and writers Hone Tuwhare, Witi Ihimaera and Patricia Grace. There has been a parallel growth in the work of Pacific Island New Zealanders such as artists Fatu Feu'u, Lily Laita and Ani O'Neil and novelists Albert Wendt and Sia Figiel. Maori art combines traditional and contemporary images, while Pacific Island New Zealand artists often feature experiences of immigration and influences of their island heritage as major themes in their work.

Above: *A Maori man with a traditional facial tattoo, or moko, in Koru patterns.*
Opposite: *The altar of the Roman Catholic church at Jerusalem, on the Whanganui River, featuring traditional Maori carvings and wall panels.*

THE KORU

The koru is a stylized fern-scroll motif traditionally used in Maori carving and tattooing. Taken from the bunched, unfolding branch of the ponga tree, the koru is also commonly used as a contemporary emblem, most conspicuously on the tail of Air New Zealand's planes.

Above: *The distinctive All Black shirt and scarf both have the silver fern symbol.*

Sport

A mild climate, abundant recreation areas and an admiration for physical excellence have made New Zealanders **ardent sports people** who have had international success in rowing, rugby, netball, squash, softball, cricket, horse riding and yachting.

The leading men's winter sports are **rugby union**, which New Zealanders are passionate about, rugby league, soccer and hockey. Even the smallest New Zealand town has a rugby field. Under the professional system introduced in 1995, the rugby union season begins in February with the international Super 12 competition and concludes with the National Provincial Championship final in late October.

The legendary **All Blacks** play annual internationals against traditional rivals Australia and South Africa as part of the Tri-Nations Series, as well as competing against France, England, Ireland, Scotland and Wales. The loss of an important test match by the All Blacks has been known to cause an onset of national depression among New Zealand rugby followers.

Rugby league, soccer, netball, women's rugby and touch have grown in popularity in recent years. The ski season lasts from June to October, and indoor sports include squash and badminton. New Zealand's golf courses occupy some of the loveliest land in the country.

The most popular summer sports are **cricket** – men's and women's – tennis, athletics and sailing. Rowing competitions take place on inland lakes such as Karapiro in the Waikato. Triathlons and 'Iron Man' contests attract many competitors. The long coastline and warm conditions allow **swimming** in most regions from mid-November to May, but board riding and wind-surfing are enjoyed throughout the year with the added comfort of wet suits. Surf lifesaving championships are held every summer.

Sea fishing is a hugely popular pastime, both from boats and shore, while fishing for rainbow and brown trout in New Zealand's cooler lakes and rivers attracts both local and overseas visitors.

Funding for Sport

Sport and Recreation New Zealand (SPARC) was formed in 2002, following the merger of the Hillary Commission, the New Zealand Sports Foundation and the policy arm of the Office of Tourism and Sport. This government-funded body helps sport by assisting the thousands of volunteer coaches, umpires and team managers who actively support sport in New Zealand. Web: www.sparc.org.nz

Food and Drink

For years New Zealand produced superb ingredients – meat, poultry, fish and vegetables – then cooked them with a lack of imagination. 'Meat and three veg', soggy salads and charred BBQ chops and sausages were the standard fare, and foreign food was viewed with suspicion.

Those days are over. Now the ingredients are matched by the treatment they receive from food professionals. New Zealand's **new cuisine**, a mélange of overseas recipes and local influences, is as tempting and tasty as any in the world, and is complemented by locally produced wines of exceptional quality. Pastoral products such as lamb and beef, a variety of seafoods and a climate which enables most vegetables to grow most of the year round are the foundations of a thriving and diverse food industry.

Venison, mussels, salmon, lamb, scallops, snapper, crayfish, oysters and whitebait – not the overseas variety but the larvae of the native trout – provide the basis of some of New Zealand's most distinctive main courses, while delicious desserts utilize the many varieties of fresh fruits available, often combined with farm-fresh dairy products.

Stylishly served with a Marlborough Chardonnay or Sauvignon Blanc, or a Hawke's Bay Cabernet Sauvignon, and followed by locally made cheeses of peerless quality, a meal in a reputable New Zealand restaurant can be a memorable experience. There are also now more than 50 wine and food festivals held throughout New Zealand, most of which take place in February and March.

Regional Specialities

While there are regional specialties, such as West Coast whitebait, Bluff oysters, Canterbury lamb, South Island farmed salmon and Kaikoura crayfish, New Zealand chefs enthusiastically adopt foods from all parts of the country. An efficient transport system means that foods produced in one area can be marketed the next day anywhere else in the country, retaining that hallmark freshness. A new generation of chefs, many with overseas experience, a re willing and able to experiment with new varieties of fruit and vegetables, resulting in unique culinary creations.

Left: *This wine shop at Akaroa on the Banks Peninsula offers a choice of local vintages.*

2
Auckland, Northland and the Coromandel

New Zealand's largest city by far (with a population of 1,100,000), **Auckland** sprawls across the **Tamaki Isthmus**. Called 'The City of Sails' after its large collection of yachts, it is a maritime city which looks to the sea in all directions: the **Waitemata Harbour** and **Hauraki Gulf** to the east, the **Manukau Harbour** and **Tasman Sea** to the west. For all Aucklanders the sea in its many moods is a constant presence. It is estimated that there are between 80,000 and 90,000 leisure boats in Auckland.

Auckland was chosen as New Zealand's capital by Governor **William Hobson** in 1840 (named after his patron, the First Earl of Auckland). The settlement soon became a trading centre, growing around the Waitemata Harbour, but lost its capital status to Wellington in 1865. Today it extends 40km (25 miles) north to south and its suburbs sprawl west to the Waitakere Range and east to Waiheke Island.

Basking in a mild, maritime climate and blessed with beaches, accessible islands and regional parks, Auckland has attracted thousands of **overseas migrants**. The city is sometimes derided by those from other parts of the country, who view it and its inhabitants as brazen, hedonistic and uncultured. Aucklanders are bemused rather than offended by this judgement: after all, most residents have moved to the city from elsewhere in New Zealand.

Auckland is the **world's largest Polynesian city**, with 20 per cent of its people being Maori, Samoan, Tongan, Cook Island or Niuean. Recent migration from south and east Asia, eastern Europe and South Africa have added extra cultural elements to this vibrant, cosmopolitan city.

Don't Miss

*** **The War Memorial Museum and Domain:** a neoclassical building set in the verdant domain, the museum contains a collection of Maoritanga, Polynesian and Melanesian artefacts.
*** **Rangitoto Island:** a 600-year-old volcanic island guarding the entrance to Waitemata Harbour; majestic views and walking tracks.
** **The Sky Tower:** on a clear day the views from the observation decks provide a panoramic view of Auckland.

Opposite: *Devonport, Waitemata Harbour and central Auckland as seen from Mount Victoria.*

Above: *The Sky Tower, with its viewing decks and revolving restaurant, in central Auckland.*

CLIMATE

Auckland's climate is strongly affected by the city's **maritime** location. Extremes of temperature are unknown: **summers** are warm and humidity often high; **winters** mild and wet. There are few days without wind, but frosts are rare. Most spectacular are the occasional spring and summer deluges, when sudden, brief downpours of **subtropical rain** drench the city. However the warm and mostly clear days from December to April enable Aucklanders to revel in boating, barbeques, outdoor concerts and beach activities.

AUCKLAND CITY SIGHTSEEING

A trip to the top of the **Sky Tower** provides a spectacular introduction to the city and its surrounding region. It is also possible to bungy jump from near the top of the tower. From the observation decks and revolving restaurant at 328m (1075ft) many of the isthmus's 49 volcanic vents can be clearly seen. These extinct **basaltic cones** stud the area, the most obvious being Mount Eden, One Tree Hill, Mount Hobson, Mount St John and Mount Albert, while across the harbour Mount Victoria and North Head are the twin crowns of Devonport. The cones are reserve land, so that they stand up like green pyramids amid the city's suburbia. Guided walks can be taken across the upper arch of the harbour bridge, from where there are panoramic views of the city and the Waitemata Harbour.

Another way to see Auckland is to take the **ferry to Devonport**, a Victorian seaside village on the **North Shore**. The trip across the harbour takes only 11 minutes, but provides a water view of the business district, harbour, harbour bridge and hinterland. At the Devonport end, a walk up the main street and a short steep climb to the summit of **Mt Victoria**, at the top of the street, gives an even better appreciation of Auckland's aquatic activities. Yachts, launches, ferries, container ships and cargo vessels ply the waters constantly, and Mt Victoria and **North Head**, at the entrance to the inner harbour, provide panoramic views of the Waitemata Harbour, the city and its marinas. The **Visitor Information Centre** in Devonport, near the harbour end of the main street, Victoria Road, specializes in advice for visitors to the North Shore.

A Central City Walk ***

The city's main thoroughfare, **Queen Street**, and the Downtown area at the foot of it, are two of its least memorable features, but next to it, on the eastern side, are delightful districts to explore on foot. A good place to begin is on the corner of **Vulcan Lane** and **Queen Street**, the fourth corner on the left up from QE II Square.

From Vulcan Lane, turn right into **High Street**. This district is a blend of boutiques, bookshops, bars and cafés. From here it is just a short walk up Victoria Street East and Bowen Street to Princes Street and the **University of Auckland**. At the north of the campus, its entrance marked by a gatehouse and surrounded by gardens, is **Old Government House** (1856), one-time residence of the Governors of New Zealand, and now the university's Senior Common Room.

Across Princes Street from the university clock tower is **Albert Park**, an oasis of formal gardens, lawns and fountains. In the southwestern corner of the park is the **Auckland Art Gallery**, and across Kitchener Street is the New Gallery, which features more modern art.

A short walk down Wellesley Street East and across Queen Street is **The Edge**, a modern complex containing the **Aotea Centre**, the Force Entertainment Centre, Borders Bookstore and, on the corner of Queen Street and Wellesley Street West, the superbly restored Art Nouveau theatre, the **Civic**, built in 1929.

The walk continues up Queen Street, past Aotea Square and the old Town Hall and, where the street steepens, a row of Oriental food shops and cafés to **Karangahape Road**. Take a right turn here. Known as **'K-Road'**, this street is a colourful mixture of old-fashioned apparel shops, coffee bars, pubs, cafés, night-clubs, restaurants and, at its western end, strip clubs and massage parlours. K-Road is Auckland's bohemian fringe.

Walking back down Pitt Street and Hobson Street towards the Sky

FROM PACIFIC TO TASMAN

One of the most satisfying Auckland **walks** is the coast-to-coast, 4-hour, 13km (8-mile) hike across **Tamaki Isthmus**. It begins at the Ferry Building, on the **Waitemata Harbour** (an arm of the Pacific Ocean) and ends at Onehunga on the shores of **Manukau Harbour** (an inlet of the Tasman Sea). The route, which is well sign-posted, takes the walker right across the North Island. Along the way it passes some of Auckland's most prominent landmarks, including **The Domain**, **Mount Eden** and **One Tree Hill**, so the coast-to-coast walk is an excellent way to become acquainted with the city.

EATING OUT

Major hotels have their own restaurants, but a good way to get to know the city is to sample the ones away from the hotels. Most eateries are in Ponsonby Road, Jervois Road, Parnell Road and Victoria Road, **Devonport**. Most are licensed or bring-your-own wine (BYO). Also try Vulcan Lane and High Street in the central city. Restaurants are plentiful on the **waterfront**, especially on Princes Wharf. There are two in the restored Ferry Building, in Quay Street, and at Westhaven, beside the harbour bridge. All have views of the inner harbour. Two eastern suburbs, **St Heliers** and **Mission Bay**, also feature waterfront dining. **Broadway**, Newmarket, has a number of cafés and restaurants, and a first floor food hall in front of the Rialto cinema complex.

Tower brings you to the **Sky City complex and casino**, at the base of the tower. From there it is a short downhill walk to the Viaduct Harbour, a harbourside complex built for New Zealand's defence of the America's Cup in 2000. Apartments, restaurants, bars, cafés and an auditorium, attract throngs of visitors during the summer months, from December through March. New Zealand lost the America's Cup early in 2003 to a Swiss syndicate.

The **National Maritime Museum**, beside the entrance to the village, has fascinating displays of New Zealand's long seafaring history, both Polynesian and European. Sheltered moorings in front of the museum accommodate traditional and modern sailing vessels. At the end of the walk, refreshments can be obtained from the many bars and restaurants overlooking the harbour on **Princes Wharf**.

AROUND AUCKLAND

Some of the best attractions are found within an hour's drive or ferry ride from central Auckland. It is a 20-minute drive to the tree-clad, hillside suburb of Titirangi. From there **Scenic Drive** follows the crest of the **Waitakere Ranges**, an ancient volcanic ridge covered in native bush which offers spectacular views back to the city. Be sure to call at the **Arataki Visitor Centre**, on Scenic Drive, which contains comprehensive information about the area.

Two main roads run off Scenic Drive to the coast: Piha Road and Bethells/Te Henga Road. A spur road from the Piha Road descends steeply to Karekare Beach. **Karekare**, **Piha** and **Te Henga** are all dramatic, unspoiled beaches on Auckland's west coast. Backed by the Waitakere Ranges and pounded by huge Tasman waves, the beaches make for wonderful walking. There are also many tramping tracks through the Waitakeres.

Further north is **Muriwai Beach**, off SH16. It, too, is rugged and spectacular, and has the added attraction of a gannet colony, atop two rocky

Below: *The Maritime Museum on the waterfront, Waitemata Harbour.*

outcrops at the southern end of the beach. The return drive, through Waimauku, Huapai and Kumeu, passes some of the region's best-known **wineries**, all of which offer tastings and cellar sales.

A word of warning: the West Coast's pounding waves, tidal rips (undertows) and hidden holes make **swimming hazardous**. There have been many fatalities here. Only swim in those areas patrolled by **life guards**, between the yellow-and-red flags. Even when beach walking, keep a close eye out for **rogue waves** which have a habit of sweeping unexpectedly up the sand, carrying all before them.

Above: *A busy waterfront bar in the Viaduct Basin, central Auckland.*

Special Attractions ***

Kelly Tarlton's Antarctic Encounter and Underwater World, on the eastern waterfront, is an outstanding attraction. Built underground, in disused sewage holding tanks, Kelly Tarlton's exhibits enable the visitor to imagine the hardships of the early Antarctic explorers through lifelike recreations, and to view a colony of King and Gentoo Penguins from a slowly moving snow-cat. Visitors are taken on a moving walkway through a 110m (120yd) plexiglass tunnel, over which sharks, stingrays, snapper, hapuka and many other species of fish glide. It is like taking a comfortable stroll along the ocean floor.

Auckland Zoological Park, just off the Northwestern Motorway, houses over 600 animals. It is home to tuatara and kiwis, as well as orang-utans, meerkats, hippos, lions and giraffes. 'Pridelands' and 'Hippo River', recreations of an African savannah and wetland, provide a spacious natural habitat for the zoo's African animals.

Separated from the zoo by Western Springs park is the **Museum of Transport, Technology and Social History**, known commonly as **MOTAT**. This is a rather eccentric but diverting collection of old cars, planes, steam engines and other contraptions, and a reconstruction of a colonial village street. On the other side of the zoo is the **Sir Keith Park Memorial Site**, where restored World War II planes and flying boats are housed in a hangar.

Auckland's Markets

Near the city centre is the **Victoria Park Market**, at the end of Wellesley Street West. It specializes in crafts and clothing. There is a market in **K-Road** on Saturdays from 10:00–16:00. The **Otara Market** in the town car park operates on Saturday mornings from 05:00–12:00. At the **Mangere Town Centre** the market is on Saturdays and Sundays. West Auckland's largest market is held at the **Avondale Racecourse** on Sunday mornings, while on the North Shore there is a Sunday morning market in **Takapuna**'s car park.

Right: *A takahe, one of New Zealand's rarest flightless birds that was long thought to be extinct, ranges freely on Tiritiri Matangi Island in the Hauraki Gulf.*

> **ISLAND SANCTUARIES**
>
> **Tiritiri Matangi**, off the end of the **Whangaparaoa Peninsula**, 30km (18.5 miles) north of Auckland, is a predator-free 'open sanctuary' for many of New Zealand's endangered birds. In a **reforestation** programme, hundreds of native trees were planted, creating a natural habitat for **takahe**, **stitchbirds**, **saddlebacks**, **little spotted kiwi** and **kokako**. Bush walkways enable visitors to watch the birds. For details tel: (09) 476 0010, website: www.tiritirimatangi.org.nz There are ferries to the island from Gulf Harbour Marina, on the Whangaparaoa Peninsula, and from Auckland City. **Little Barrier Island**, whose profile can be seen from Auckland, is not open to visitors as it is a **nature reserve** and breeding environment for New Zealand's endangered birds, including the **kaka**, **kokako** and **stitchbird**.

Hauraki Gulf ***

The Hauraki Gulf, east of Auckland City, is a boat-lover's paradise. Most of the many islands in the gulf make up the **Hauraki Gulf Marine Park**, which was enshrined in government legislation in 2000, and are open to the public. The islands provide sheltered anchorages, sandy beaches and fine walks, while the gulf itself offers excellent sailing, cruising and fishing. Access to the islands can be on private pleasure craft or via regular ferry services.

Rangitoto guards the entrance to the Waitemata Harbour. It is Auckland's newest volcano and its lava landscape is one of raw natural beauty. The climb to the cone, through stands of pohutukawa, is uplifting in every way. There are a few baches (small holiday cottages) on the island, but they are disappearing as their leases are not permitted to be renewed.

Motutapu, joined to Rangitoto by a causeway, is completely different from its volcanic neighbour. It is not volcanic, and its landscape consists of gently rolling hills and grassland, with a network of pathways, the remains of World War II military installations, an elevated coastline and a fine beach and picnic site at Home Bay.

Motuihe is popular with daytrippers and fishermen. It has two excellent sandy beaches on either side of its narrow isthmus, so that one is always sheltered from the wind, and there are walking tracks through the native bush.

Brown's Island is a tiny, contoured volcanic cone only a mile from the mainland. Covered in grass, the flat land on the island's southern side makes a fine picnic spot.

Waiheke, 40 minutes' fast ferry ride from Auckland, is a large island of rolling hills, groves of native bush, small settlements and superb beaches, notably Oneroa, Onetangi and Mawhitipana Bay (Palm Beach). Waiheke's microclimate – drier than the mainland – makes it ideal for red grape growing, and Waiheke labels, like Goldwater Estate and Stoneyridge, are some of the most respected in the country.

Once a retreat for 'alternative lifestylers', Waiheke today has a substantial commuting population seeking an escape from the city. Most people live at the western end of the island; the central and eastern parts are hilly, open farmland. Stony Batter, a huge World War II gun emplacement at the eastern end of the island, provides wonderful views of the gulf.

Great Barrier Island is a large island of volcanic origin, 90km (56 miles) northeast of Auckland and connected by a fast ferry service. 'The Barrier' has a mountainous interior, native forest, indented harbours and superb beaches on its eastern coast. The relative isolation, tranquillity and easy-going way of life on Great Barrier make it a peaceful haven for those wanting to get away from it all.

On the flanks of Great Barrier's **Mount Hobson** are the remains of wooden dams that were used to impound the rivers, then 'tripped' to flush kauri logs to the coast. They were then rafted and floated to sawmills for processing.

The largest settlement on Great Barrier is **Tryphena**, but there is also basic accommodation at Whangaparapara and Fitzroy. There are air services from Auckland to the island's airfields at Claris and Okiwi.

A Diving Mecca

The **Poor Knights Islands**, offshore from Whananaki, is one of the world's finest dive locations. A marine reserve, the two large and several smaller islands have exceptionally clear waters which abound with marine life. Visibility is up to 30m (98ft) for most of the year, although plankton make the water murky from Oct–Dec. Vertical rock faces drop nearly 100m (328ft) to the sandy ocean floor, and contain arches, caves and fissures which are home to a multitude of fish, shellfish and soft corals. It is forbidden to land on the islands, which are the preserve of prehistoric lizards, tuataras, geckos and skinks. Visit by charter boat from Tutukaka.

Below: *A typical bay on Waiheke Island, where the coastline includes sheltered coves and sandy beaches.*

The Story of the Kauri

The **Kauri Museum** at Matakohe 45km (28 miles) south of Dargaville, is one of the most interesting in New Zealand. Its dramatic displays show how the felling, transportation and milling of kauri trees defined the colonial history of Northland and nearby Kaipara Harbour for several decades. Another valuable industry was digging for fossilized kauri gum, in northern swamplands. The gum was carved into ornaments or used as an industrial raw material for making varnish. The museum has a large collection of kauri gum on display.

Northland

The northwest trending 350km (217-mile) peninsula that is Northland begins at Warkworth and extends to North Cape. It is a fascinating region with a **subtropical climate**, a rich history and a strong sea presence. The **Aupouri Peninsula** from Awanui to Cape Reinga is known as the **Far North**. It is spectacularly beautiful, and the turbulent meeting place of the Tasman Sea and the Pacific Ocean, clearly visible from the cape, is awe-inspiring.

Northland's **two coasts** are distinctly **different**. The west coast is straight and swept by powerful, wind-driven breakers, although there are several deeply indented harbours; the east coast is sheltered and contains beautiful bays, islands and golden beaches. Averaging only 60km (37 miles) wide, the peninsula can be quickly crossed to savour the attractions of the contrasting coasts.

In Maori legend, the great Polynesian explorer **Kupe** discovered the Hokianga harbour after his voyage from the spiritual homeland of Hawaiiki. Settlement followed. Early Maori found the mild climate, the many harbours and the abundance of fish and birds ideal for their existence.

Opposite: *Cape Reinga, in Maori legend the departing place of the spirits.*

New Zealand's European settlement also began in this region. After European contact, the **whalers**, **traders** and **missionaries** made Northland their base. Kororareka, now Russell, in the Bay of Islands, was a rather rumbustious capital town by the 1830s; nearby Waitangi was the site of the signing of the treaty between many Maori chiefs and British colonial authorities in 1840. In 1844 there were serious conflicts here between Maori warriors and the British troops, and later in the 19th century

Northland's extensive kauri forests were plundered and the land converted to pastures.

Northland is a region of diverse natural and cultural appeal where tourism is very well developed. **Paihia**, in the Bay of Islands, is the tourist hub from which various excursions can be taken. Boat charters ensure comfortable explorations of the Bay of Islands, while the land attractions are ideal for self-drive excursions or coach tours.

As well as the well-known attractions of Northland, there are many delightful minor surprises to be found here, such as the dazzling white silica sands of the Parengarenga Harbour entrance, the exquisite cove of Matai Bay, the craft shops of Kerikeri, the historical provenance of the 1830s mission house at Waimate North, and walking tracks to Cape Maria Van Diemen.

Ninety Mile Beach *

This inaccurately named beach – it's actually about 90km (56 miles) long – is a stretch of beautiful coast on the west of the Aupouri Peninsula. You can drive to **Cape Reinga** on the hard sand below the high-tide mark, or take a coach tour. The latter is recommended, as the drivers are aware of tides and the sinking sands of the Te Paki stream bed, which must be negotiated near the beach's northern end. Kaitaia is the nearest place from where a coach tour leaves. Ninety Mile Beach is home to the endangered shellfish delicacy, the burrowing toheroa, and also the location of the world's largest beach fishing contest every February.

In Maori legend **Cape Reinga**, or 'place of leaping', is the point from which the spirits of the dead leap when they leave for Hawaiiki, the spiritual home of Polynesian people. A track leads past a picturesque lighthouse to the cape, a point of grandeur and undeniable presence, heightened by the tumultuous coming together of the Tasman Sea and the Pacific Ocean. Cape Reinga is a breathtaking place, more than just a spectacular landform.

LAST RESTING PLACE OF THE *RAINBOW WARRIOR*

In 1985 the **Greenpeace** flagship *Rainbow Warrior* was sunk in Auckland harbour by French saboteurs before it could sail for French Polynesia to protest against French nuclear testing at **Mururoa Atoll**. A Greenpeace photographer on board was killed. The *Rainbow Warrior* was later towed to **Matauri Bay**, in Northland, and scuttled off **Motutapere**, one of the **Cavalli Islands**. Today the wreck is a popular dive site. A memorial to the *Rainbow Warrior*, by New Zealand sculptor Chris Booth, incorporating the vessel's propeller, stands on the hill overlooking Matauri Bay.

Above: *Tane Mahuta, or Lord of the Forest – New Zealand's mightiest kauri in the Waipoua Forest.*
Opposite: *Urupukapuka, largest island in the Bay of Islands, Northland.*

Waipoua Forest Sanctuary **

Waipoua Forest Sanctuary, on State Highway 12, is the largest remaining **kauri forest** in New Zealand, its 9000ha (22,230 acres) containing about 300 types of native trees and plants as well as the remnants of the once-extensive Northland kauri forests. The mature kauri are found in the western area of the forest, mostly single trees surrounded by taraire, northern rata, towai and rewarewa. Tane Mahuta, 'the Lord of the Forest', is the largest kauri of all, a 51m (167ft) giant over 1200 years old whose first branch is 12m (39ft) above the ground.

Trounson Kauri Park, 17km (10.5 miles) southeast of Waipoua, contains another stand of mature kauri, as well as an attractive camping ground. There are walking tracks through the forest to giant kauri trees, the most distinctive of which is the 'Four Sisters', a tree with four stems.

Approximately 20km (12 miles) to the northwest of Waipoua, **Hokianga Harbour** is an inlet of the Tasman Sea, which extends deep into the western Northland Peninsula. The entrance to this historic harbour is its most impressive aspect. Deep blue water, a perilous bar and an entrance guarded by the **mountainous golden sand dunes** of North Head can all be viewed from the promontory of South Head. Tobogganing on the dunes is exhilarating. Further inland, the shores of the Hokianga are lined with mangroves, punctuated by tiny settlements. This part of the Hokianga is literally a backwater, with negligible employment now that timber milling and farming have declined. The tiny village of Kohukohu, on the harbour's northern shore, is connected to the town of **Rawene**, on the opposite side, by ferry.

HONE HEKE'S FLAGSTAFF

Above **Russell** is the historic flagstaff on **Maiki Hill**. In 1844–45, Ngapuhi chief Hone Heke four times cut down the flagstaff flying the Union Jack, in defiance of British colonial authority. The present flagpole was cut from the original lower mast and erected in 1858 by the descendants of Heke's warriors.

The Bay of Islands ***

The Bay of Islands is one of New Zealand's pre-eminent tourist centres, an extensive complex of sheltered beaches, peninsulas, capes and bays, all within easy reach of the area's two main towns, **Paihia** and **Russell**. Paihia is the more functional of the two, a base for exploring the district offering all types of accommodation, plus land and water tours, including day cruises to the islands and swimming with dolphins. North of Paihia is the restored **Treaty House**, home of the early British resident, James Busby, and site of the signing of the Treaty of Waitangi on 6 February 1840, and an imposing *whare runanga*, or Maori meeting house. Russell, just across the bay by passenger ferry, is more picturesque, historic and the headquarters of the Bay of Islands' game-fishing industry. A short walk across the hill behind the town is Oneroa Bay, a sheltered and safe swimming beach.

Feeding the Fish

For those who are fascinated by marine life but lack scuba skills or equipment, **Goat Island Marine Reserve**, near Leigh, offers the chance for **snorkellers** to swim among the fish. Established as a marine reserve in 1975 and named after the small island just offshore, the clear water teems with snapper and blue maomao, and crayfish inhabit the holes in the reserve's reef. The fish will take food from visitors' hands so readily that the practice is now prohibited because they are becoming aggressive in their feeding. It's best just to swim a few metres from the beach, then float with mask and snorkel among the fearless fish.

Cities and Towns *

The only city in Northland is **Whangarei** which, even though it lacks major attractions in itself, is a useful base for exploring the coastal district east of the city. New Zealand's only oil refinery, Marsden Point, stands on the southern head of Whangarei's large harbour, and from Bream Head 491m (1610ft), on the northern side, there are views of the Hen and Chickens Islands. The drive east from Whangarei passes through attractive countryside to three of the most appealing seaside settlements in the region: **Ngunguru**, **Tutukaka** and **Matapouri Bay**. Tutukaka is a sheltered harbour and game fishing base, while Matapouri Bay and nearby Sandy Bay are superb beaches.

Warkworth, the centre of the Kowhai Coast, is an attractively situated town in the south of Northland. Built on the Mahurangi River, which is navigable to the centre of the

town at high tide, Warkworth becomes a busy centre for holidaymakers from December to March. The waters of the Mahurangi Harbour, below the town, are excellent for sailing and cruising all year, and are also handy to picturesque **Kawau Island**. Ferries to Kawau leave regularly from Sandspit, ten minutes' drive from Warkworth. The Matakana district, a few kilometres east of the town, has some fine vineyards, as well as the Morris & James pottery and tileworks, which incorporates a café within its premises. Parry Kauri Park, on the outskirts of Warkworth, contains nature trails and some majestic, ancient kauri trees.

Hot Water Beach

A side road from SH25 leads to the settlement of Hot Water Beach, named after the heated water that emerges from the sand at low tide at the foot of a towering cliff. Here you can dig your own hot pool in the sand, and the beach's thermal waters attract hordes of visitors throughout the year. The ocean at Hot Water Beach offers excellent body and board surfing, but there is also a strong undertow which makes caution essential when swimming.

The Coromandel

A mountainous, 100km (62 miles) long **peninsula** fringed with sandy beaches, the Coromandel is a popular holiday destination as well as having a sizeable permanent population. Its spine is remote and forested, covered with the remnants of kauri forests which were milled ruthlessly in pioneer times, and regenerating bush. A goldrush in the 1860s also ravaged some of the landscape as the quartz gold was sought. Mercury Bay was named by English explorer Captain James Cook when he observed the transit of the planet Mercury from the bay on 9 November, 1769.

Today the Coromandel has many conservation-minded inhabitants and is the centre of the **Green political movement** as well as home to many craftspeople. The peninsula is rugged in the interior and particularly beautiful along its eastern coast, where there are several fine surfing beaches and many sheltered inlets, bays and estuaries, all backed by bush-covered ranges or pine plantations.

The road along the western side of the peninsula hugs the coastline from Thames to Port Jackson. From Thames to Coromandel the road has fine views over the Firth of Thames, but becomes rough for the last 20km (12.5 miles) as it passes

beneath the lofty **Moehau Range**. On the eastern coast of the peninsula the road winds around the estuaries and through holiday towns such as **Whangamata**, **Tairua**, **Whitianga** and **Kuaotunu**. Along the way there are stunning, gold-sand beaches, crystal-clear water, and sublime views of the **Alderman** and **Mercury** islands, which seem to float off-shore on the sparkling blue Pacific. It is not possible to drive right around the northern extremity of the peninsula, although there are four steep, winding roads which cross it.

The main towns of the Coromandel on its western side are **Thames**, where the history of gold-mining can be seen at the Thames Gold Mine and Stamper Battery, and **Coromandel** itself, a smaller settlement where there are many craft shops and colonial buildings. About 3km (2 miles) north of the town is the marvellous **Driving Creek Railway and Potteries**, the creation of local potter, Barry Brickell, a working pottery and narrow-gauge railway which takes passengers through stands of re-generating native forest.

On the east coast, **Whangamata** is a resort and service town with a fine surfing beach, Tairua and nearby Pauanui are holiday towns on either side of a pretty estuary and **Whitianga**'s small population swells dramatically during the summer as holiday-makers descend on the town to enjoy its beaches. Some of the most delightful attractions of the Coromandel, however, lie in its hidden niches, such as the Opoutere estuary, the Kauaeranga Valley and Lonely Bay.

Above: *The view from Mercury Island Reserve, eastern Coromandel coast.*
Opposite: *A waterfall in the Coromandel Forest, near Whitianga.*

Cathedral Cove

Above Hahei, near Whitianga, a 5km (3-mile) walking track begins. From a lookout platform and information board, the track winds up and down coastal hills, to **Cathedral Cove**, a spectacular rock formation of white cliffs and a natural archway beside a sandy bay. The track offers fine views of **Mercury Bay**, while the cove is a perfect picnic and swimming spot. The walk takes about an hour.

Auckland, Northland and the Coromandel at a Glance

Best Time To Visit

January–April. Summer is hot, though sea breezes temper the heat. Resorts are busy in January, but after the school holidays the crowds diminish. February–March is the period of long hot days. Swimming is possible well into April.

Getting There

Auckland International Airport is 20km (12.5 miles) south of the central city. The international terminal is near the **domestic** one, which has frequent connecting flights to the rest of New Zealand. A walkway and free bus connect the two terminals. Between 06:25 and 10:05 the **Air Bus** leaves from both terminals every 20 minutes and calls at main hotels along the way. Small **Shuttle buses** ply the airport to city route, their routes varying at passengers' requests. There are taxi ranks and major **rental car** companies at both terminals.

Getting Around

Public transport in Auckland is mainly **bus**; **trains** run between the new Britomart Transport Centre and Waitakere in the west, and Papakura in the south. The Tranz Scenic train to Wellington leaves Auckland Station at 08:30 and 20:40, daily. **InterCity coaches** connect Auckland to most of the North Island, leaving from Sky City building, Hobson St; reservations, tel: (09) 913 6100. **Stagecoach Buses** connect suburbs and city. Most leave from and arrive at Britomart Transport Centre, between Quay and Customs streets. For Auckland buses and trains, call **Rideline**, tel; (09) 366 6400. The **Link Bus** is a frequent, cheap circuit of central Auckland, between Downtown and Newmarket, 06:00–18:00 Mon–Fri. For NZ$8 an **Aucklandpass** offers all-day use of all Stagecoach Auckland buses, Link buses and cross-harbour Link ferries. Buy it on a Link bus, Stagecoach bus or at the Link ferry ticket office. A free bus, **City Circuit**, circuits central city streets, starting and ending at Britomart every 10 minutes from 08:00–18:00 daily. There are regular **ferry links** to Devonport, Bayswater, Birkenhead, and Half Moon Bay. The terminal is across Quay St from QEII Square, at the bottom end of Queen St.

Where to Stay

Auckland

Luxury

The Heritage, 35 Hobson St, Auckland, tel: (09) 379 8553, fax: (09) 379 8554, e-mail: res.heritageakl@dynasty.co.nz web: www.dynasty.co.nz Beautifully restored former department store; few minutes' walk from Viaduct Harbour.

Esplanade Hotel, 1 Victoria Rd, Devonport. Edwardian (1903) charm and elegance, on the waterfront across from the Devonport ferry terminal, tel: (09) 445 1291, fax: (09) 445 1999, e-mail: reservations@esplanadehotel.co.nz web: www.esplanadehotel.co.nz

Stamford Plaza, Albert St, tel: (09) 309 8888, fax: (09) 379 6445 (general), (09) 303 0583 (reservations), web: www.stamford.com.au Near America's Cup village.

Quality Motels

Cornwall Park Motor Inn, 317 Manukau Rd, Epsom, tel: (09) 638 6409, fax: (09) 638 6407, website: www.cornwallpark-motorinn.co.nz Near Newmarket.

Parklane Motor Inn Takapuna, cnr Lake Rd and Rewiti Ave, Takapuna, tel: (09) 486 1069, fax: (09) 486 2658, web: www.parklane.co.nz Near motorway and harbour bridge.

Budget

Aspen House, 62 Emily Place, tel: (09) 379 6698, e-mail: aspenhouse@xtra.co.nz web: www.aspenhouse.co.nz Central city, near waterfront.

Northland

Mid-range

Pacific Rendezvous, above Tutukaka, tel: (09) 434 3847, reservations: 0800 999 800, fax: (09) 434 3919, e-mail: pacific@igrin.co.nz web: www.oceanresort.co.nz

The Duke of Marlborough Hotel, 35 The Strand, Russell, tel: (09) 403 7819, fax: (09) 403 7828, e-mail info@theduke.co.nz web: www.theduke.co.nz A refurbished historic, waterfront hotel.

Auckland, Northland and the Coromandel at a Glance

Coromandel

MID-RANGE

Admirals Arms Hotel, 146 Wharf Rd, Coromandel, tel/fax: (07) 866 8272, e-mail: nyden@paradise.net.nz web: www.admiralsarms.co.nz Fully refurbished, historic hotel.

WHERE TO EAT

Most of Auckland's restaurants are in Ponsonby Rd and Jervois Rd, Parnell Rd, Vulcan Lane and High St, the Viaduct Basin, Princes Wharf, on the waterfront at Mission Bay and in Victoria Rd, Devonport.

Auckland

LUXURY

Antoine's Restaurant, 333 Parnell Road, Parnell, tel: (09) 379 8756. Offers high quality cuisine and wines.

White, end of Princes Wharf, within Hilton Hotel. Stylish dining; delightful views of the harbour, tel: (09) 9782020, e-mail: fbauckland@hilton.com web: www.hilton.com

MID-RANGE

MaiThai, 1st floor, cnr Albert St and Victoria St West, tel: (09) 303 2550. Thai food; considerate service; private dining rooms available.

Cin Cin on Quay, Ferry Building, 99 Quay St, tel: (09) 307 6966. On the harbour edge, with bars that overlook Quay St and the water.

TOURS AND EXCURSIONS

Fullers Cruises provide cruises in modern, comfortable ferries to Rangitoto, Waiheke, Kawau, Motuihe and Great Barrier Islands. Fullers office is in the Ferry Building on Quay St. Day cruises direct to Coromandel town and its historic hinterland are available from Kawau Kat, in the Viaduct Harbour. Web: www.kawaukat.co.nz

Just in front of the National Maritime Museum you can take a cruise of 45 minutes to 2½ hours on the Waitemata Harbour, on a 50m yacht from the **Pride of Auckland** fleet. Every ticket on a Pride yacht includes free entry to the Maritime Museum.

In **Northland** are **Dolphin Discoveries Eco Tours**, NZ Post Building Paihia, and Swordfish Club Building, Russell, tel: (09) 402 8234, fax: (09) 402 6058, web: www.dolphinz.co.nz Cruises leave twice daily from Paihia and Russell. Discover the Bay of Islands and swim with dolphins.

Sand Safaris, 221 Commerce St, Kaitaia, tel: 0800 86 90 90, fax: (09) 408 3339, web: www.sandsafaris.co.nz Safaris to Cape Reinga via 90 Mile Beach and Te Paki Stream. Specialize in small groups (up to 28).

USEFUL CONTACTS

Auckland's Travel and Information Centres provide free, impartial advice on all aspects of Auckland and New Zealand travel. Open daily, at SkyCity, cnr Victoria and Federal streets, and Viaduct Harbour, cnr Quay and Hobson streets; tel: (09) 979 2333. On Waiheke Island there is the Waiheke Visitor Information Centre at 2 Korora Rd, 'Artworks', Oneroa, and on Great Barrier Island the Great Barrier Visitor Information Centre is at Claris Airport. Auckland's website is: www.aucklandnz.com

In **Northland** is **Information Far North**, PO Box 262, Jaycee Park, South Rd, Kaitaia, tel: (09) 408 0879, fax: (09) 408 2546, booking line: 0800 363 463, e-mail: visitorinfo@fndc.govt.nz

Bay of Islands Information, Marsden Rd, Paihia, tel: (09) 402 7345, fax: (09) 402 7314, booking line: 0800 363 463, e-mail: visitorinfo@fndc.govt.nz web: www.twincoast.co.nz

AUCKLAND	J	F	M	A	M	J	J	A	S	O	N	D
AVE. MAX TEMP. °C	23	24	23	20	18	15	15	15	17	18	20	22
AVE. MAX. TEMP. °F	73	75	73	68	64	59	59	59	63	64	68	72
AVE. MIN TEMP. °C	16	17	16	13	11	9	8	9	10	11	13	15
AVE. MIN TEMP. °F	61	63	61	55	52	48	46	48	50	52	55	59
AVE. RAINFALL mm	79	94	81	97	125	137	145	117	102	102	85	85
AVE. RAINFALL in	3.1	3.7	3.2	3.8	4.9	5.4	5.7	4.6	4.0	4.0	3.3	3.3

3
The Central North Island

This region is one of tremendous geographic diversity: plains, mountains, lakes, volcanoes, forests, farmland, beaches and a cold desert. It contains some of New Zealand's finest scenic attractions, most of which are less than three hours' drive apart. It extends from the inland city of **Hamilton** in the north, to the active volcanic mountain zone of **Tongariro National Park** in the south, from remote, wave-beaten, **black sand beaches** of the west coast to the grand sweep of the **Bay of Plenty** in the east, where there are reportedly endless, golden sand beaches and beachside towns, backed by highly productive horticultural land. Off the eastern coast stands the active volcanic landmark, **White Island**, whose steam plume can usually be seen emerging from its crater on a fine day.

Within these boundaries lies some of New Zealand's most fertile pastoral land, the region of the **Waikato**, which is drained by the North Island's longest river. From the Waikato the land rises steeply to the broad zone of the **Volcanic Plateau**, which contains some of the world's most active and spectacular volcanism, the mighty **Lake Taupo**, and the famed tourist town, **Rotorua**. Here the Earth's crust is perilously thin. Escaping through the crust, superheated water emerges as steam, geysers, hot springs and pools, and beneath it the earth is melted to boiling mud. Exotic **pine forests**, planted during the depression of the 1930s, occupy vast tracts of land across the plateau, while one of the North Island's largest remaining native forests, **Pureora**, lies to the west of Lake Taupo.

DON'T MISS

*** **Mount Maunganui beach:** excellent conditions for swimming, boogie boarding and board-riding.
*** **Rotorua:** geo-thermal wonderland of geysers, mud pools and volcanic craters.
*** **Tongariro National Park:** volcanic mountains, native forests and lakes.
** **Lake Taupo:** take a drive along the lake's eastern shore from Taupo town to Turangi.
** **Waitomo Caves:** a mysterious subterranean world of glow-worms, grottos, caverns and rivers.

Opposite: *Pohutu Geyser, Whakarewarewa, sends a plume of steam skywards.*

THE ERUPTIONS OF RUAPEHU

Ruapehu has erupted several times, most notably in 1945. The most recent eruptions were in 1995–96. On 23 September 1995 a plume 12km (7.5 miles) high threw rocks 1.5km (0.9 miles) from the crater and generated lahars (mud flows) in three valleys. In June–July 1996 eruptions sent ash over 300km (186 miles) from the mountain. The ash showers created a hazard which closed airports and cut short ski seasons, affecting the income of many in nearby National Park and Ohakune dependent on visitors to the ski fields. The eruptions were the costliest in New Zealand since Mount Tarawera in 1886.

The crowning geographic feature of the central North Island is the trio of lofty volcanic mountains, **Tongariro**, **Ngauruhoe** and **Ruapehu**, which are visible on a clear day from a great distance. In summer, or when they are swathed in snow in winter, these mighty volcanoes utterly dominate the landscape. New Zealand's only cold desert lies to the east of Mount Ruapehu.

HAMILTON AND THE WAIKATO

Hamilton (166,128), capital of the rich Waikato farming region, is New Zealand's fourth largest city, a transport hub and one of the country's only sizeable inland cities. Built on the banks of the **Waikato River**, the city has a more relaxed atmosphere than Auckland, just under two hours' drive away to the north.

The Waikato, with high banks on either side, flows through the city. There are pleasant **walkways** along the riverbanks, and lunchtime, afternoon or evening cruises can be taken on the river on the paddle steamer *MV Waipa Delta*. Also on the river bank is the excellent **Waikato Museum of Art and History**, while **Hamilton Gardens**, at the southern end of the city alongside SH1, is a lovely botanical feature. **Hamilton Zoo** has a large walk-through aviary. The city's cafés and bars are mainly at the South End, on or around Victoria Street, the main thoroughfare. Just south of Hamilton is **Mystery Creek**, known for its popular agricultural field days.

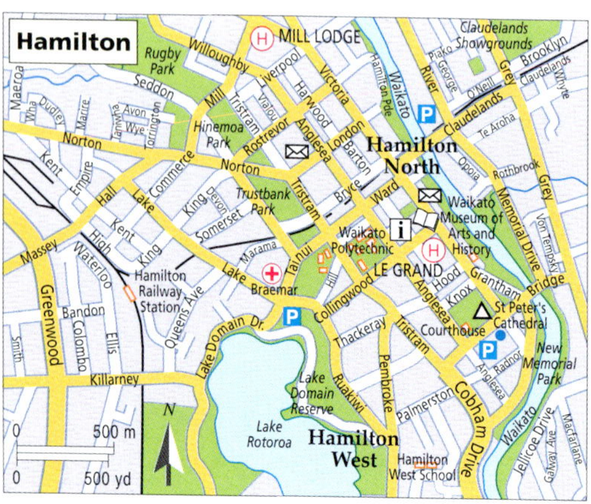

Surrounding the city are the undulating hills and **lush pastures** of the Waikato region, centre of the highly successful New Zealand **bloodstock industry** and the country's most productive **dairy farming** land. The centre of horse-breeding is the district surrounding the

leafy town of **Cambridge**. Several stud farms welcome visitors. The centre of New Zealand rowing is **Lake Karapiro**, on the Waikato River near Cambridge.

North of Hamilton, at the junction of Waikato and Waipa rivers, is **Ngaruawahia**, home of Maori Queen, Te Arikinui Dame Te Atairangikaahu, and centre of the **King Movement**, a force of Maori nationalism since 1858. The countryside near Matamata, east of Hamilton, was the location for Bilbo Baggins' home of Hobbiton, in the first of the film adaptations of the *Lord of the Rings* trilogy.

Above: *Rolling green hills dominate the rural landscape near the Waitomo Caves, Waikato region.*

The holiday town of **Raglan**, 48km (30 miles) west of Hamilton, has a picturesque harbour, black sand beaches and classic point breaks at Manu Bay and Whale Bay, which have made it a Mecca for surfers. The **Waitomo Caves**, off SH3 between Otorohanga and Te Kuiti, offers an awe-inspiring, subterranean world of glow-worm caves, blackwater rafting and abseiling.

Tauranga, Mount Maunganui and the Bay of Plenty Coastline

This is one of New Zealand's premier holiday areas, a sun-drenched, fruit-growing district with golden beaches and sparkling seas. The coastline appears to curve away to infinity, extending as it does from Mount Maunganui, east to Cape Runaway, 170km (105 miles) away.

Tauranga (101,000) is the country's fastest-growing city, yet it retains its relaxed, holiday atmosphere, built as it is over a finger of land extending into a wide, sheltered **harbour**. The city is connected by a harbour bridge 3.5km (2 miles) long, to nearby **Mt Maunganui** 232m (761ft). 'The Mount', as it is known locally, caps the end of a *tombolo* (a long sandy peninsula) and overlooks the narrow entrance to Tauranga Harbour and neighbouring **Matakana Island** on one side and a beach noted for its **fine surfing** on the other. There are superb views of Tauranga and the Bay of Plenty from the summit of the steep-sided Mount.

Mayor Island

This cone-shaped volcanic island, known as Tuhua by Maori, lies 40km (25 miles) off the coast from Tauranga. For early Maori the island was a vital source of obsidian, or volcanic glass, for making cutting tools. Pieces of obsidian were flaked off from blocks of the substance and used as knives.

Today, day trips can be taken to the island from Tauranga or Mount Maunganui. The waters around Mayor Island are noted for their big game fishing. Marlin, shark and tuna are the most common species caught. Fishing charters operate out of the marina in Tauranga Harbour.

Right: *The crater of White Island, New Zealand's most active volcano, smoulders off the coast of the Bay of Plenty.*
Opposite: *This Maori craftsman is hard at work on a wood carving.*

East of Papamoa in the Bay of Plenty, SH2 swings inland to pass through the prime **kiwifruit** growing districts around the town of **Te Puke**, the 'kiwifruit capital of the world', then returns to the coast for a time before turning inland and passing through the hinterland of **Whakatane**, a quiet town built on a shelf of land beneath a hill on the south side of the Whakatane River mouth. A pleasant 4km (2.5 miles) walkway leads from Pohaturoa Rock, a site sacred to Maori in the centre of Whakatane, to the top of the hill and out to Kohi Point.

Just to the east of Whakatane is **Ohope**, one of New Zealand's loveliest beaches, and a little further along the coast, the holiday settlement of **Opotiki**, the easternmost town in the Bay of Plenty.

WHITE ISLAND

New Zealand's most continuously active cone volcano is situated 50km (31 miles) off the Bay of Plenty coast, near Whakatane and Opotiki. The volcano had a sulphur mine within its crater in the late 19th and early 20th centuries, until an eruption killed several miners. White Island's large crater floor is littered with volcanic rubble and sulphur-encrusted fumaroles (steam vents). Day trips to the spectacular island can be taken by sea or helicopter from Whakatane.

ROTORUA

For over 160 years Rotorua ('Two Lakes') has been the heart of tourism. Victorian travellers were as fascinated by its natural wonders as visitors are today. It is also the spiritual heartland of the **Te Arawa people**, the place where traditional **Maori culture** can be most readily experienced.

In Rotorua and its surrounding districts the forces of volcanism are seen at their most dramatic. Geysers, boiling mud pools, scalding hot lakes, mineral hot pools, belching vents, sulphurous odours, a buried village, and a volcanic chasm are all highly accessible, joining less restless natural attractions such as crystal-clear trout streams and forest-rimmed lakes. Visitors can also 'take the waters' in the European spa tradition.

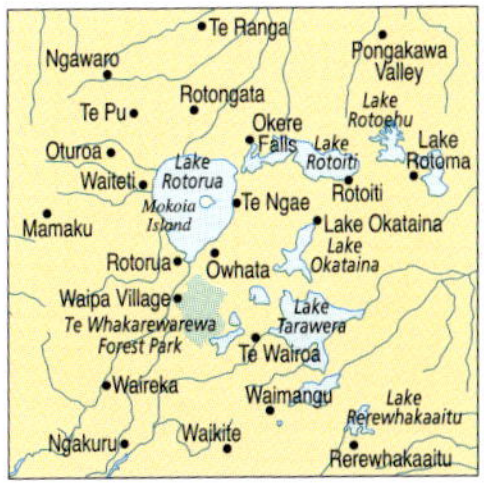

Rotorua is also a trout fisherman's delight. The lakes, streams and rivers of the region abound with **rainbow trout**, and the angling is made even more attractive by the bush-fringed settings. The Ohau Channel, which connects Lakes Rotorua and Rotoiti, is a particularly attractive stretch of angling water. For those who prefer just to observe the fish, **Rainbow Springs**, 4km (2.5 miles) to the northwest of Rotorua, offers crystalline streams and glass-sided trout viewing pools, surrounded by native forest and forest paths.

Maori cultural performances and **earth-oven food** can be sampled at the major hotels or through a number of package deals. **The Agrodome**, about 5km (3 miles) to the northwest of the town, features entertaining farm animal activities, including sheep shearing, while for the more adventurous, **whitewater rafting** on the Kaituna River, which flows north out of Lake Rotoiti, provides a short, exhilarating ride.

The Legend of Hinemoa and Tutanekai

Mokoia Island, in Lake Rotorua, is the setting for the best-known Maori legend. A young maiden, Hinemoa, lived on the lake shore; Tutanekai, who lived on the island, fell in love with her. She was higher born than he, and their love was forbidden. One night, on hearing Tutanekai's flute music wafting across the lake, she could not resist and, with the aid of gourds, swam out to the island. She warmed herself in a hot pool, where she was found by Tutanekai, and their love was consummated. Today, Mokoia Island is popular with visitors wishing to see Hinemoa's Pool, as well as a native bird sanctuary.

Government Gardens *

The Government Gardens are located on a level area of land extending into Lake Rotorua. Formally laid out in the Victorian manner, the gardens nevertheless betray their volcanic underlay by exuding steam from numerous vents in the grounds. The neo-Tudor bathhouse, Rotorua's most imposing building, is reminiscent of a traditional European spa and today accommodates the town's **Museum of Art and History** as well as the restored and preserved old bathhouse itself. South of the museum, in Hinemoa Street, is the **Polynesian Spa**. Here there are hot thermal pools of several types and sizes, whose waters are said to be beneficial for sufferers of rheumatism or arthritis. The famous **Blue Baths** have been restored to their original glory.

The Eruption of Mount Tarawera

During the night of 10 June 1886, people in the Rotorua area were awoken by strong earthquakes. Tourists who had come to view the Pink and White Terraces, one of the great natural wonders of the world, were among those who were woken by the unsettling earth movements. Suddenly a huge black cloud, illuminated by lightning and fireballs, burst from Mount Tarawera, 25km (15.5 miles) southeast of Rotorua township. A massive volcanic eruption was under way. It split the mountain asunder, spewing out ash and lava, opening a chasm 17km (10.5 miles) long, burying the village of Te Wairoa, other Maori settlements and the Pink and White Terraces beneath mud and ash, killing an estimated 153 people.

Whakarewarewa The Thermal Reserve ★

Just 2km (1.2 miles) south of the Rotorua town centre, this district is a landscape of silica-encrusted rocks, steaming pools, bubbling grey mud and erupting geysers, crossed by pathways. King of the geysers is mighty **Pohutu**, whose eruptions hurl hot water 30m (98ft) into the air.

Incorporated in the reserve is a **living Maori village** and a replica of a traditional one. Beside the reserve is the **Maori Arts and Crafts Institute**, where Maori artisans can be seen carrying out traditional carving and weaving activities and instructing the young in these arts.

Hell's Gate, Tikitere, 15 minutes' drive east of Rotorua on SH30, is the district's most dramatic thermal reserve: a landscape of scalding hot pools, fumeroles (steam vents) boiling mud pools, a sulphurous lake and a hot water cascade. Tempering the effects of these features are lovely stands of native forest. Other impressive geothermal districts are found to the south of Rotorua town in the **Waimangu thermal valley**, which was created by the 1886 eruption of Mount Tarawera, and at **Wai-o-Tapu**.

Mount Tarawera ★

Now dormant, Mount Tarawera, at 1111m (3644ft), can be visited on foot, by 4WD vehicle, or by plane or helicopter. The crater is about 17km (10.5 miles) long, a 300m (984ft) deep gash across the mountaintop, littered with volcanic rubble and coloured with ochre and sulphur-yellow hues of exposed volcanic sub-strata.

Sometimes given the name 'New Zealand's Pompeii', **Te Wairoa**, the buried village, was certainly subjected to the same titanic forces when nearby Mount Tarawera erupted on 10 June 1886. Showers of ash engulfed the village, which has now been excavated and partly reconstructed. There is a small museum containing artefacts from the village and paintings of the lost Pink and White Terraces. There is also an attractive bush walk and waterfall nearby.

Left: *Fishing for trout in the crystal-clear waters of Lake Taupo, the largest lake in the country.*
Opposite: *The magnificent crater of Mount Tarawera was created by the great eruption of 1886.*

Taupo

Lake Taupo was created after a cataclysmic volcanic eruption 1800 years ago. Hot ash and pumice rock ejected by the eruption covered 20,000km^2 (12,400 sq miles) of the North Island and the skies as far as China and Rome were affected. Natural drainage subsequently filled the huge crater, creating New Zealand's **largest lake**, 369m (1282ft) above sea level. Lightweight pumice rocks still litter the shores of the lake. Taupo and its tributary rivers comprise one of the best-known **trout fishing** areas in the world.

There are magnificent views from the north across the lake to the volcanic peaks of **Tongariro National Park**, particularly the perfect cone of Mount Ngauruhoe. **Taupo town**, a popular holiday centre, is built around the shores of **Acacia Bay**, in the northeast corner of the lake. The mighty **Waikato River** begins its journey to the sea after it flows from Lake Taupo on the western edge of the town.

The lake is most **accessible** from SH1, which follows its eastern shores closely, and from the waterfront at Taupo town. There are excellent views from this road and many attractive **picnic areas** along the way. The western road, SH32, is some distance from the lake, although spur roads lead to the shore at Kuratau and Omori, at its southwestern end. The lakeside areas are very popular with Aucklanders and Wellingtonians for holidays and weekends away.

Trout

The brown trout *(Salmo trutta)* is a member of the salmon family and was introduced to New Zealand from North America in the 1880s. They migrate upstream to breed, several times during their lifetime, then make their way back down again, feeding and growing in deep river pools and lakes. The less common rainbow trout *(Salmo gairdnerii)* lives primarily in Lake Taupo and spawns in its tributary streams and rivers. Taupo is renowned for its rainbow trout. The largest recorded trout caught in the lake weighed just over 8kg (17.6 lb). Trout cannot be farmed or harvested in New Zealand, and Taupo is one of the last true wild trout fisheries in the world.

Above: *A wildwater canoeist negotiates the turbulent waters of the Huka Falls.*
Opposite: *Mount Ruapehu, a live volcano, is also the North Island's highest mountain.*

Attractions around Taupo **

Taupo town clusters along the shores of the lake at its northeastern end. There are many motels south of the town, while the shopping centre, cafés and restaurants are at the western end, close to where the Waikato River flows from the lake.

Cruises can be taken on the lake, during which several picturesque landmarks can be visited, including Whakaipo Bay, Karangahape Cliffs and Motutaiko Island. For those who wish to **fish from the lake**, boats of many kinds are available for charter from the boat harbour, with skippers who know the best place to catch the big one.

Just north of town is **Huka Falls**, a dramatic cataract formed by the swift-flowing river as it surges through a granite cleft, then plunges over an 11m (36ft) shelf. **Huka Lodge**, upstream from the falls, is one of New Zealand's most exclusive fishing lodges. Guests can fish the river, just a stroll away from their luxury accommodation. About 3km (1.8 miles) further north is the district of **Wairakei**, which has one of New Zealand's finest golf courses, a geothermal power station, and Craters of the Moon, a 30-minute walk around steaming craters and boiling mud pools. **Orakei Korako**, a hidden valley of colourful silica terraces and spouting geysers reached by shuttle boat across the Waikato River, is located 40km (25 miles) north of Taupo, east of SH1.

There are several **thermal pools** in the area. The best is **De Bretts Thermal Resort** at the southern end of town, near the start of the Taupo-Napier road (SH5). In an attractive valley are two large outdoor pools, one hotter than the other, and several private mineral pools. Just north of Taupo is **Spa Thermal Park**, with hot bathing pools and a bushwalk which can be combined with a riverbank walk to Huka Falls, 4km (2.5 miles) away.

A Mountain of Legend

Mount Hikurangi is the North Island's highest non-volcanic mountain and one of the very first on Earth to receive the rays of the sun each new day. Hikurangi is held in deep reverence by the Maori. Legend has it that the mountain is the last resting place of the canoe of **Maui**, the Polynesian ancestral fisherman. From this canoe Maui caught the great fish, **Te Ika-a-Maui**, which became the North Island.

The crystal-clear rivers which flow into Lake Taupo are a joy for **fly fishermen**, especially March–September when mature rainbow trout swim up the tributaries to spawn in the shallow waters upstream. One of the finest rivers is the **Waitahanui**, 13km (8 miles) south of the town on SH1. Both the river and the short stretch of water where it flows into the lake offer superb fly fishing. The **Tongariro River**, which flows through a delta and into the lake at its southern end, has several world-famous fly-fishing pools such as Admirals, Major Jones and The Duchess. For those who wish to get close to nature, fly fishing guides are available to take anglers into isolated stretches of river to find the elusive trout. A fishing licence is necessary. To savour the fish in a different way, a visit to the **Tongariro National Trout Centre** on SH1, 5km (3 miles) south of Turangi, shows the way trout are bred and the fry nurtured before being released into streams and rivers all over the country.

LORD OF THE RINGS

In 1999 New Zealand film producer Peter Jackson began filming J.R.R. Tolkien's *Lord of the Rings* trilogy. Outdoor locations for the films included **Matamata** in the Waikato (Hobbiton), **Tongariro National Park** (slopes of Mt Doom) and **Queenstown** (summit of Amon Hen), showcasing many of New Zealand's spectacular landscapes. The final, Oscar award-winning film in the trilogy, *The Return of the King*, premiered in Wellington in 2003. Some of the film's locations can be visited. Queenstown's **Dart River Safaris** visit **Paradise**, which features in the first of the trilogy. New Zealand as 'Home of Middle-Earth' can be visited at www.purenz.com

TONGARIRO NATIONAL PARK

Centred around a trio of volcanic peaks, **Ruapehu** 2797m (9174ft), **Tongariro** 1967m (6451ft) and **Ngauruhoe** 2291m (7514ft), Tongariro National Park is one of the few areas in the world with **dual World Heritage Status**, a recognition of its natural and cultural importance. It is a unique wilderness area with beech forests, tussock grasslands, wetlands, active volcanoes, volcanic lakes, lava formations and hot springs. In summer its **tramping tracks** draw thousands of hikers, in winter it is the North Island's premier **ski region**. Horse trekking, rafting, caving, canoeing, trout fishing and mountain biking are also possible within the park.

The three volcanoes are distinctly different in character and appearance. **Ruapehu**, the largest, is a massive cone volcano with several peaks, a crater 1.5km (0.9 miles) wide and a hot

THE UREWERAS AND LAKE WAIKAREMOANA

About 90km (56 miles) inland from Gisborne is **Te Urewera National Park**, the most extensive area of untouched indigenous forest in the North Island and home of the **Tuhoe** people. Here the mountains of the Huiarau Range are densely forested, inhabited by feral pigs and deer and crossed by swift-flowing streams and tramping tracks. **Lake Waikaremoana** occupies a natural basin in the park. Enclosed by native forest, its shores are surrounded by white sand beaches, waterfalls and spectacular bluffs, and its waters are cool and clean. There are also several top-class walking tracks around the lake.

lake within it, ice cliffs and deep gullies carved into its slopes. **Ngauruhoe** is an almost perfectly shaped volcanic cone which has been built up by successive eruptions of andesite from its central vent, while **Tongariro** has several craters, some recent, some ancient.

The Attractions of Tongariro National Park **

The **Tongariro Crossing**, a one-day hike, is one of the most spectacular in New Zealand. During the approximately eight hours it takes to do the hike, the track ascends a valley and valley head, crosses the broad floor of a volcanic crater, passes around the rim of a volcano, descends alongside emerald and blue lakes, through tussock grassland to the **Ketetahi Hut**, and concludes after passing through a stand of native bush. Along the way there are spectacular **views** of the **volcanic mountains** and lakes Rotoaira and Taupo.

The crossing begins at the Mangatepopo hut, a short bus ride from Whakapapa village on the slopes of Mount Ruapehu, and ends at a car park on the Ketetahi Road. The crossing can be done in either direction, but the shuttle buses which deposit and collect hikers do so on the basis of a Mangatepopo to Ketetahi traverse.

Below: *Tama Lakes, volcanic explosion craters along the Tongariro Crossing.*

Mount Ruapehu contains the North Island's two main ski fields, **Turoa** and **Whakapapa**, on the western side of the mountain. A much smaller one, **Tukino**, is situated on its eastern slopes. During the time when the snow comes, usually in July to mid-October, thousands of skiers from all over the North Island make the journey up the mountain.

Whakapapa has a dozen chair lifts and T-bars and more than 30 groomed runs; Turoa has wide, groomed trails which include the longest vertical ski-drop in New Zealand at 720m (2362ft).

Whakapapa's nearest après-ski is the tiny village of **National Park**. Near Turoa ski field, on the southern side of Mount Ruapehu, is the township of **Ohakune**, which offers the best après-ski. Ohakune also revels in its market gardening status as the 'Carrot Capital' of New Zealand. One to five-day guided tours of Whanganui National Park can also be taken from Ohakune. Access to the much smaller **Tukino** ski-field is by 4WD, from the Desert Road side of the mountain.

At **Waiouru**, New Zealand's main army base at the southern end of the Desert Road, is the **QEII Army Memorial Museum**, which contains displays commemorating the nation's military heritage from colonial to modern times.

Above: *A tranquil river valley in the Whanganui National Park.*

The Whanganui River

Although it is not the longest river in the North Island, the Whanganui is a waterway of great historic and recreational significance. Its main source is the slopes of **Mount Tongariro**. After cutting through the tussock flats of Tongariro National Park the upper Whanganui flows west, becoming a sizeable river by the time it passes the King Country town of **Taumarunui**. It then turns sharply south and flows on a winding course, through a gorge, over rapids and past several tiny riverside settlements until it reaches the sea at the provincial city of Wanganui.

Maori tribes found the Whanganui a valuable **access-way** to the interior of the North Island by means of canoes, which they poled and paddled upstream. The first Europeans travelled up the river in 1831, and from the 1840s **missionaries** used it to reach the Maori tribes who lived along its banks. The river became a focus of the Maori nationalist movement, the **Hauhau**, in the 1850s and 1860s. By the early 1900s travelling up the Whanganui on steamers and houseboats was a leading tourist attraction.

Today the river remains significant to the Maori living along its banks. There are important **marae** at settlements like Ranana, Koriniti and Pipiriki, and river

The Bridge to Nowhere

After World War I, returning soldiers and their families tried to establish farms in the remote **Mangapurua Valley**, which contains a tributary of the Whanganui River. Beaten by isolation and economic hardship, the settlers had largely abandoned the land by the 1920s. Nevertheless, a bridge 41m (134ft) above the valley was opened in 1936, but the government refused to make funds available for road maintenance and the **bridge was cut off**. Today it remains an object of curiosity, known as The Bridge to Nowhere, reached from the Whanganui River or by the Mangapurua Track.

Above: *Jerusalem, a mission settlement beside the Whanganui River.* **Opposite:** *A pastoral landscape in the fertile East Coast region.*

people are linked through the Whanganui River Maori Trust Board. The Whanganui National Park was established in 1987, recognizing the area's unique and extensive natural landscapes. The park borders the river, its area totalling 74,231ha (183,350 acres).

About half of the roads are now sealed and so it is possible to drive up the river. The best way to appreciate the river's tranquil beauty, however, is from the water, and the Whanganui is popular with **canoeists**. There are many **walking tracks** here, such as the Mangapurua Track at 40km (25 miles) long, and the Matemateaonga Track at 42km (26 miles), which links the Whanganui River to Taranaki.

Wanganui is built on both banks of the river and is a service centre for sheep and cattle farmers in the surrounding area. The central city's Victorian buildings have been restored and the streets paved with cobblestones. The **Whanganui Regional Museum** and nearby **Sarjeant Art Gallery** provide the city's cultural highlights, while Virginia Lake, north of the city by St Johns Hill, is a lovely restful area. The Durie Hill elevator, built in 1919, ascends the hill, on the south bank of the river, to its summit.

Castlecliff is Wanganui's seaside suburb. Like most west coast beaches, Castlecliff's is exposed and turbulent, its sands littered with driftwood washed along from the mouth of the Whanganui River just a short distance away.

MOTHER AUBERT

The Roman Catholic order **Daughters of Our Lady of Compassion** was founded in 1892 at the settlement of **Jerusalem** by a French-born nun, **Mother Mary Aubert** (1835-1926). In the 1880s and 1890s she also published a significant Maori text, and manufactured and sold herbal remedies. St Joseph's, the Catholic church at Jerusalem, still stands above the river.

The famous New Zealand poet, **James K Baxter** (1926–1972) also made Jerusalem his home for the last three years of his life, attracting a community of followers. His tombstone, made from a single river stone, carries his Maori name, Hemi.

THE EAST COAST AND POVERTY BAY

The East Coast is a shoulder of land protruding from the New Zealand mainland's easternmost extremity, culminating at **East Cape** (178° 35′ E). It is an isolated and lightly populated area, with no town of any size between Whakatane in the Bay of Plenty and Gisborne in Poverty

Bay, but the road follows the coastline for most of the way, affording fine ocean views. Inland is the rugged Raukumara Range and the region's highest point, **Mount Hikurangi** 1754m (5753ft).

The hill land is used mainly for **pastoral farming**, and transport by horseback is common. The East Coast has a high percentage of Maori people, and life in tiny settlements like **Hicks Bay**, **Te Araroa**, **Tikitiki**, **Tokomaru Bay** and **Tolaga Bay** is determinedly unhurried. Many of the bays contain superb sand beaches. The most notable man-made landmarks are the long wharf at Tolaga Bay and the lovely old Church of England at Tikitiki, the interior of which contains some fine Maori design features.

Gisborne is the first city in the world to see the light of the new day, a distinction made much of during the 2000 millennium celebrations. It is also a place of great historical significance, for it was on the shores of Poverty Bay, or Turanga-nui as Maori called it, that members of Captain James Cook's expedition came ashore on 8 October, 1769, the **first Europeans** to set foot in New Zealand.

Cook named the area **Poverty Bay** because it provided his expedition with few supplies, but in fact its soils are fertile and the sunny climate make it one of New Zealand's **most productive lowlands**, where grape vines and food crops thrive. Gisborne itself is a quiet city with wide streets, an obelisk marking Captain Cook's landing place near the city's river mouth and a statue of the navigator on Kaiti Hill, above the city.

The area around Gisborne has some fine **boutique wineries** and good **beaches**, including Midway and Waikanae beaches close to the town centre, and Wainui, just east of the city. New Zealand's most extensive collection of introduced trees is found at Eastwoodhill Arboretum, about 35km (22 miles) southwest of Gisborne.

The Pacific Coast Highway

This highway follows the Pacific Coast of the North Island from Auckland to Napier. It has superb ocean vistas along the way, including the eastern Coromandel, the whole coastline of the Bay of Plenty, the East Coast, Poverty Bay and Hawke Bay. Towns with much visitor appeal, such as Thames, Tairua, Mount Maunganui and Opotiki, punctuate the marine drive. Details of the highway can be obtained on the website www.PacificCoastNZ.com

> **THE DAIRY PROVINCE**
>
> Taranaki is dairyland, and the milk from its cow herds goes to make various high-quality dairy products. **Dairyland**, on the outskirts of Hawera in south Taranaki, offers visitors an insight into the dairy industry, with diverting displays of production processes, a virtual reality milk tanker ride through the dairying countryside and a revolving restaurant complete with milking plant and cow bails. Dairyland, cnr Whareroa Rd and SH3, Hawera, tel: (06) 278 4537, fax: (06) 278 5735.

TARANAKI

Taranaki province occupies the bulge on the western coast of the North Island. Its landscape is dominated by the 2518m (8465ft) gullied volcanic cone, **Mount Taranaki** (also known as Mount Egmont) and its subsidiary cone, Fanthams Peak 1966m (6448ft). A ring plain of fertile farmland surrounds the mountain, while to the east of it is heavily dissected hill country. The province's only city, **New Plymouth**, lies on the northern coast. Taranaki is New Zealand's 'energy province', and the deposits of **natural gas and oil** which lie beneath the ring plain make a substantial contribution to the nation's **energy** needs.

Mount Taranaki is easily accessible from the eastern and southern sides. Three good roads ascend the mountain from Inglewood, Stratford and Kaponga, leading to North Egmont, East Egmont and Dawson Falls respectively. There is an abrupt change from pastures to native forest as the roads pass into **Egmont National Park**. The upper slopes of the mountain are usually coated in snow from May through to October. Two mountain lodges, one Swiss-style, offer comfortable accommodation.

A variety of tracks cross the mountain, from a short walk to Dawson Falls to a 3–5 day tramp right around the mountain, and a guided summit climb. From the summit

Above: *The impressive volcanic cone of Mount Taranaki, viewed from its surrounding native forest.*

are views to the Tasman Sea in the west and over the hill country to the Volcanic Plateau to the east. The more adventurous can hire a guide and try rock climbing, abseiling, mountaineering or extreme skiing.

It is only a 45-minute drive from the mountain to the Taranaki coast. '**Surf Highway 45**', runs from New Plymouth to Hawera and passes some premium surfing spots, including Weld Road, Stent Road and Opunake. The coast is a Mecca for surfers, featuring point breaks and glassy waves in the right conditions. There are also excellent surf beaches at Oakura and Opunake.

Taranaki's fertile volcanic soils and high rainfall produce many luxuriant gardens. The most notable is **Pukeiti**, a rainforest garden 20km (12.5 miles) from New Plymouth, between Pouakai and Kaitake. It has the largest collection of rhododendrons and azaleas in New Zealand, and their vibrant blooming from August–November is a dazzling sight.

New Plymouth lies beside an exposed coast. A new 6.8km (4.2 mile) coastal walkway offers many features, including three beaches and a 45m (150ft) tall kinetic sculpture called Wind Wand. At the western end of the walkway is the **Sugar Loaf Marine Reserve**. This consists of several volcanic remnants, the highest of which is Paritutu. It is possible to cruise among the Sugar Loaf Islands and visit a seal colony there.

The main attractions in town are the **Govett Brewster Art Gallery**, the award-winning museum and library complex, **Puke Ariki**, and **Richmond Historic Cottage**. **St Mary's Pro Cathedral** in Vivian St, begun in 1845, is New Zealand's oldest stone church. Near New Plymouth's main street is **Pukekura Park**, which specializes in native species in a setting of lakes and fountains. The annual Festival of Lights, held in the park in December, is popular. Adjoining the park is a cricket ground and **Brooklands**, a formal park of gardens, lawns and trees. Brooklands Bowl is a natural amphitheatre used for concerts and festivals in summer.

The Legend of the Mountains

Maori legend has it that long ago the volcano of Taranaki stood alongside t he other three in the centre of the North Island. Then the mighty Tongariro and Taranaki mountains clashed over the affections of a maiden called **Pihanga**. Taranaki lost, and in grief and anger fled recklessly towards the setting sun, tearing a deep wound in the earth behind him. A stream of clear water sprang from Tongariro to heal the wound and forests grew beside the new river, which became known as the **Whanganui**.

The Central North Island at a Glance

Best Times To Visit

Summer (January–April) is best for outdoor activities on the coast, Lake Taupo and the Volcanic Plateau. **Autumn** (April–June) is cool and dry, and in **winter** (July–September) Mount Ruapehu is the North Island's main snowboarding and skiing resort. The inland areas and the Volcanic Plateau can be very cold at night. Rotorua's thermal attractions make it appealing year-round.

Getting There

State Highway One bisects the region, passing through the Waikato, Hamilton, Taupo and Waiouru. The Pacific Coast Highway along the Coromandel, Bay of Plenty and East Coast is scenic, as is the Thermal Explorer Highway from Hamilton to Rotorua and Taupo on SH1 and SH5. The Volcanic Loop on SH1, SH49, SH4 and SH47, from Turangi to Waiouru, Ohakune, National Park and back to Turangi, circles the volcanic crown.

Getting Around

Regular **air** and coach services connect the major centres with Hamilton, New Plymouth, Tauranga, Rotorua, Taupo and Gisborne. Intercity and Mount Cook **coaches** ply the central North Island daily. The Overlander **train** from Auckland to Wellington stops at Hamilton, Te Kuiti, Te Awamutu, Taumarunui, National Park, Ohakune and Waiouru.

Where to Stay

As the central North Island has some of New Zealand's most popular tourist destinations, there is much accommodation, from resort hotels, motor lodges and backpacker hostels to campground cabins, homestays and farmstays.

Hamilton
Mid-range
The Ambassador Hotel, 86 Ulster St, tel: (07) 839 5111, fax: (07) 839 5104, reservations: 0800 800 533. Near sporting and recreational facilities.

Tauranga
Mid-range
Hotel Armitage, 9 Willow St, tel: (07) 578 9119, fax: (07) 577 9198, reservations: 0800 276 482, web: www.armitage.nz-hotels.com
Near central shops.

New Plymouth
Mid-range
Plymouth International Hotel & Conference Centre, cnr Courtenay and Leach streets, tel: (06) 758 0589, fax: (06) 758 9949, reservations: 0800 800 597, e-mail: plym.int@xtra.co.nz
Has sea and city views.

Taupo
Mid-range
The Lakeland of Taupo, Two Mile Bay, tel: (07) 378 3893, fax: (07) 378 3891, reservations: 0800 378 389, e-mail: info@lakeland.co.nz
web: www@lakeland.co.nz
Lake view, landscaped grounds.

Tongariro National Park
Luxury
The Grand Chateau, on the slopes of Mount Ruapehu, tel: (07) 892 3809, fax: (07) 892 3704, reservations: 0800 24 28 32, e-mail: grand.chateau@xtra.co.nz
web: www.chateau.co.nz
Built in 1929 and refurbished in 2004; one of New Zealand's most venerable hotels.

Rotorua
Mid-range
The Princes Gate, tel: (07) 348 1179, fax: (07) 348 6215, reservations: 0800 500 705, e-mail: princes.gate@clear.net.nz
web: www.princesgate.co.nz
A historical boutique hotel near the lakefront.

Gisborne
Mid-range
Colonial Motor Lodge, 715 Gladstone Rd, tel: (06) 867 9165, fax: (06) 867 4099, e-mail: colonial_motor_lodge@xtra.co.nz
Near beaches and city centre.

Wanganui
Mid-range
Rutland Arms Inn, 48–52 Ridgway St, tel: (06) 347 7677, fax: (06) 347 7345, e-mail: enquiries@rutland-arms.co.nz web: www.rutland-arms.co.nz
Close to the town bridge and styled after an old English inn.

The Central North Island at a Glance

Where to Eat

The most convenient places to eat are in the hotels, but each centre also has a satisfactory range of restaurants.

Tours and Excursions

Cruise the **Waikato River** on the *MV Waipa Delta*; tel: (07) 854 9814, web: www.waipadelta.co.nz
Waitomo Caves information and tours, Waitomo Caves Village, tel: (07) 878 7640, fax: (07) 878 6184, e-mail: waitomomuseum@xtra.co.nz
Waitomo Adventure Centre, tel: 0800 924 866, web: www.waitomo.co.nz
Bay of Plenty: White Island Tours & White Island Rendezvous, 15 Strand East, Whakatane, freephone: 0800 733 529, fax: (07) 308 0303; tours of active volcanic island.
In **Rotorua**, contact **Mount Tarawera Four Wheel Drive Tours** (08:30–13:30), tel: (07) 348 2814, fax: (07) 347 8147, e-mail: mttarawera@xtra.co.nz web: www.mt-tarawera.co.nz
Carey's Geothermal Wonderland Tour, 1108 Haupapa St, Rotorua, tel: (07) 347 1197, fax: (07) 347 1199, e-mail: careys@careys.co.nz web: www.careys.co.nz
In **Taupo**, **Windsor Charters** has trout fishing and cruising on Lake Taupo; tel: (07) 378 8738, fax: (07) 378 8748, e-mail: windsor-charters@xtra.co.nz
In **Tongariro National Park**, go on the **Tongariro Trek**, a four-day, fully guided walk through volcanic landscape, staying at the Grand Chateau. Tours run from Dec–Apr. Web: www.trek.co.nz
In **Wanganui**, **River City Tours** run canoe adventures in the national park; tel: (06) 34 87122 or 025 480 308, reservations: 0800 377 311, web: www.rivercitytours.co.nz www.bridgetonowheretours.co.nz
Cruise the **Whanganui River** on paddle steamer *Waimarie*, tel/fax: (06) 347 1863, e-mail: riverboatswanganui@clear.net.nz

Useful Contacts

Hamilton Visitor Information Centre, cnr Bryce and Angelsea streets, tel: (07) 839 3580, fax: (07) 839 3127, e-mail: hamiltoninfo@wave.co.nz web: www.waikatonz.com
Tourism Rotorua Travel Office, 1167 Fenton St, Private Bag 3007, Rotorua. Information and booking requirements for New Zealand; tel: (07) 348 5179, fax: (07) 348 6044, e-mail: info@tourism.rdc.govt.nz web: www.rotoruaNZ.com
In **Taranaki**, **Venture Taranaki**, 41 Molesworth St, New Plymouth, tel: (06) 757 9909, fax: (06) 759 5154, email: taranaki@taranakinz.org web: www.taranaki.info
The **East Coast** is covered by **First Light Tourism**, PO Box 2000, Gisborne, tel: (06) 867 2000, fax: (06) 868 1368, e-mail: info@firstlight.co.nz web: www.gisborne.govt.nz
In **Taupo**: the **Taupo Visitor Centre**, 30 Tongariro St, tel: (07) 376 0027, fax: (07) 378 9003, e-mail: taupo@thinkfresh.co.nz web: www.laketauponz.com and **Destination Lake Taupo**, web: www.thinkfresh.co.nz
Ruapehu is covered at the **Ruapehu Information Centre**, tel: (06) 385 8427, web: www.ruapehu.tourism.co.nz and at **Destination Ruapehu**, 15 Miro St, Ohakune, tel: (06) 385 8364, web: www.destinationruapehu.com
Wanganui Visitor Information Centre, 101 Guyton St, Wanganui, tel: (06) 349 0508, fax: (06) 349 0509, e-mail: info@wanganui.govt.nz has information on excursions to Whanganui National Park;
Turangi Visitor Centre, Ngawaka Place, Turangi, tel: (07) 386 8999, fax: (07) 386 0074, web: turangivc@laketauponz.com

TAUPO	J	F	M	A	M	J	J	A	S	O	N	D
AVE. TEMP. °C	23	23	22	18	14	12	10	12	15	16	19	22
AVE. TEMP. °F	73	73	72	64	57	54	50	54	59	61	66	72
AVE. RAINFALL mm	60	110	100	120	90	100	110	90	70	90	70	120
AVE. RAINFALL in	2.4	4.3	4.0	4.7	3.5	4.0	4.3	3.5	2.8	3.5	2.8	4.7

4
The Lower North Island

This region, although not as physically dramatic as the central North Island, has many attractive features, both rural and urban, natural and cultural.

The Hawke's Bay and Wairarapa areas include some of New Zealand's best pastoral and horticultural districts, while Wellington, the nation's capital, is one of its most sophisticated cities. There are also many safe swimming beaches along the Kapiti Coast, northwest of Wellington.

Hawke's Bay

Hawke's Bay is a sheltered lowland and a productive **horticultural** region, based on fertile alluvial soils and high sunshine hours. The bay itself, called **Hawke Bay**, faces the Pacific and is bounded by two promontories, Mahia Peninsula in the north and Cape Kidnappers to the south.

The bay has two cities, Napier and Hastings. **Napier** is known as the '**Art Deco capital of the world**', because of its many 1930s buildings designed in Spanish Mission, Stripped Classical and Art Deco style. Napier also boasts a fine esplanade – Marine Parade – lined with Norfolk pines, a Marineland and Oceanarium, and Westshore, a sheltered beach west of the city.

Hastings, which occupies flat land 12km (7.5 miles) south of Napier, has some Spanish Mission-style buildings and is surrounded by **grape and fruit-growing** land. Before grapes became so profitable, the district produced apples, pears and peaches, crops which still proliferate near Hastings. The suburb of **Havelock North** has an appealing village ambience and some splendid vineyards.

Top Attractions

*** **Oriental Bay:** a lovely sheltered city beach with restaurants and cafés.
*** **Mount Bruce National Wildlife Centre:** observe the country's rarest bird species in their natural bush habitat.
** **Cape Kidnappers:** an accessible breeding colony of the Australasian gannet.
** **Martinborough:** a gem of a town with colonial buildings and premier wineries.
** **Red Rocks Walk:** take a coastal walk from Owhiro Bay to Sinclair Head and see the fur seals in winter.

Opposite: *Chaffers Marina in Oriental Bay, central Wellington.*

Above: *Te Mata Peak, with views of Hawke's Bay area.* **Opposite:** *A typical Art Deco building, Napier.*

Bluff Hill, 102m (334ft) high above Napier, has fine views of Hawke Bay as well as the city and harbour. The steep drive to **Te Mata Peak**, at 399m (1308ft), east of Hastings, offers a panoramic view of Hawke's Bay and the Tukituki Valley. According to Maori legend the peak is a sleeping giant, the body of a chief, Te Mata o Rongokako. Some 8km (5 miles) east of Te Mata are two excellent beaches, **Ocean Beach** and **Waimarama**.

Hawke's Bay is a leading **wine-producing** region, with conditions suitable for producing a variety of high-quality wines: Pinot Noir, Chardonnay, Cabernet Sauvignon and Sauvignon Blanc. There are over 30 wineries in the region, and many have restaurants. Visitors can tread the '**Wine Trail**' through the vineyards, while the first weekend in February is '**Harvest Hawke's Bay**', a celebration of wine and food. The Mission Estate Winery, on the outskirts of Napier, also hosts an outdoor concert with an international singing star every February.

The Napier Earthquake

On 3 February 1931, Napier and Hastings were struck by a violent earthquake. Nearly every building in the two cities collapsed, **killing 256 people**. Fallen power lines caused fires which swept through the towns, and the aftershocks continued for ten days. It was New Zealand's worst natural disaster.

There were unexpected benefits from the earthquake. The harbour bed and nearby Ahuri Lagoon were uplifted, creating 4000ha (9880 acres) of new land, and Napier was rebuilt in **Art Deco** style. Today an Art Deco walk, guided or unguided, can be taken through the city to view these classic 1930s buildings and, every February, an Art Deco Weekend celebrates Napier's unique style.

The Wairarapa

Between the rugged Rimutaka and Tararua Ranges and the Pacific Ocean is the alluvial basin known as the Wairarapa. A highly productive agricultural region, the Wairarapa is best known for its quality **wines**. The rivers flowing east from the ranges drain into Lake Wairarapa and Palliser Bay. The **Lake Wairarapa** wetlands, on the eastern side of the lake, are a bird-spotter's delight, being home to 96 bird species, five of which are endangered. The east coast is wild and undeveloped, but there are many stimulating walks in the ranges and the **Haurangi (Aorangi) Forest Park** in the south. The region's largest town is **Masterton**, but the most interesting settlement for the visitor is the restored colonial village of **Martinborough**.

Castlepoint, on the remote Wairarapa coast, is a popular camping, fishing and surfing spot. A lighthouse on a craggy bluff overlooks a beach, with a sheltered lagoon behind it. **Riversdale Beach**, some 25km (15.5 miles) south of Castlepoint, also offers good swimming and surfing.

Martinborough is a gem of a town. Founded in 1881 and set around a verdant square, many of the buildings have been carefully restored in recent years and provide fine examples of colonial architecture, most notably the elegant **Martinborough Hotel**, on the town square. There are many boutiques, cafés and restaurants in the village and plentiful cottage accommodation in the district. Martinborough is also the centre of the Wairarapa's **wine** production, and there are 20 wineries in the vicinity of the town, most of which are open for tastings. The district specializes in red grape plantings, particularly Pinot Noir.

Featherston, a small town at the foot of the Rimutaka Range, is the southern gateway to the Wairarapa. Here you will find the **Fell Engine Museum**, which houses the world's only fell engine, used to haul rolling stock over the Rimutakas from 1878 until a rail tunnel was completed in 1955. The **Featherstone Heritage Complex**, next to the museum, has displays on early settlers and the town's Japanese prisoner of war camp where, in a tragic incident in 1943, 122 Japanese prisoners were killed or wounded.

The Wairarapa is connected to the large lowland of the **Manawatu**, west of the Tararua and Ruahine ranges, by the Manawatu Gorge, which has been cut through by the Manawatu River. Near the western entrance of the gorge, **Palmerston North** is the hub of the Manawatu and an important education and research centre. The central feature of the town is 'the square', a large park with gardens, trees and fountains. **Massey University**, across the river from town, specializes in veterinary and food sciences and biotechnology.

Mount Bruce

About 30km (19 miles) north of Masterton on SH2 is the **Mount Bruce National Wildlife Centre**, a breeding centre for New Zealand's most endangered birds, including the takahe, kokako, saddleback, kiwi and tuatara. The aviaries are generously sized and set among native forest, the remnant of **Forty Mile Bush**, which once covered this part of the Wairarapa.

Lower North Island

Home of Middle-Earth

Around the Wellington region the locations for the filming of *The Lord of the Rings* included **Kaitoke Regional Park** and Fernside (Featherston), while the **Hutt Valley** became Rivendell and the River Anduin, Outer Shire, Ferry Lane, Trollshaw Forest, Weathertop Hillside and Bree Streets. Closer to the central city, filming included the woods of **Central Mount Victoria** through to **Fort Dorset** in the seaside suburb of **Seatoun**, which became Bree. Indoor sets were built in Jackson's company's studios in Miramar, Wellington, leading to the city now being nick-named, 'Wellywood'.

Wellington

Wellington (population 339,747) is defined by its magnificent harbour, which is called **Port Nicholson**. Founded in 1840 as a planned settlement and declared the capital of New Zealand in 1865, the town grew around the shores of the harbour and up the steep hills that surrounded it. A shortage of level land around the harbour's inner shores led to much reclamation, so that today's central business district lies on land that was once under the sea.

Tall wooden houses climb steeply up Wellington's hillsides, providing superb views of the harbour, the '**Green Belt**' around the city, and the distant Rimutaka mountains. The city boasts many steep steps and pathways, which not only provide shortcuts between the houses, but also afford ever-changing views of the city. A **cable car** connects Lambton Quay, in the heart of the business district, with the suburb of Kelburn, high above the harbour. The city has spread far beyond the harbour area, however, through the Hutt Valley at the northern end of Port Nicholson, and across the western hills to the suburbs of Porirua, Tawa and the Kapiti Coast.

Wellington's main function is the business of government. **Parliament House**, the Beehive (government's executive wing) and other key government departments such as the Treasury, are near the northern end of Lambton Quay. Although the civil service has been reduced in recent years, a significant proportion of the city's working population is still employed in government departments. The National Library, National Archives and Alexander Turnbull

Library are also located near Parliament. The many foreign embassies and visiting political dignitaries lend Wellington a **cosmopolitan** atmosphere, heightened by its many cafés and restaurants, particularly in the Courtenay Place district.

In the 1990s an urban redevelopment scheme revitalized the city, particularly its waterfront. The **Museum of New Zealand** – or **Te Papa** – is a popular attraction on the waterfront. A walk along the harbour front from Queens Wharf to Oriental Bay makes a delightful introduction to Wellington. A modern sports ground, the **Westpac Trust Stadium**, built on the city's former railway yards, is a new, conveniently located amenity for rugby and cricket matches. The stadium is known affectionately as 'the Cake Tin'.

Above: *Wellington's cable car climbs above Kelburn Park, providing superb views of the city and its surrounding hills.*

Katherine Mansfield Birthplace ***

The tastefully restored childhood home – depicted in some of her short stories – of New Zealand's best-known writer, Katherine Mansfield (1888-1923), the daughter of a prominent Wellington banker, is situated at 25 Tinakori Road. It is open seven days a week, from 10:00–16:00, except Christmas Day and Good Friday.

The Cable Car ***

First opened in 1902 and modernized in 1979, the single track, two-car system climbs from Lambton Quay up past Kelburn Park to the top of the Botanic Gardens, making three stops along the way – at Clifton Terrace, Talavera Terrace and Kelburn Park.

The Museum of New Zealand ***

This five-storey complex of exhibitions displays many aspects of New Zealand's history, land and different cultures, enlivened by modern technology. It is open daily from 10:00–18:00, and until 21:00 on Thursdays.

Kapiti Island

Some 6km (3.7 miles) off Paraparaumu Beach, and 50km (31 miles) north of Wellington, is the brooding hump of Kapiti Island. Bush-clad, with precipitous cliffs on its western side, the island was the fortress headquarters of the Maori warrior chief **Te Rauparaha** from 1822 until his death in 1849. Today it is a predator-free bird sanctuary where native birds such as kaka, weka, kakariki, saddlebacks, fantails, bellbirds and tui thrive among the regenerating bush. The island rises to 521m (1709ft) and can be explored via three fine walking tracks. Kapiti is administered by the Department of Conservation and day trips from Paraparaumu Beach are possible if landing permits are obtained in advance from the DOC office in Wellington.

The Lower North Island at a Glance

Best Times To Visit

The best time to visit the region is from January to April, and also from May to June when autumn days are warm and still in the eastern area. Frosts may occur between June and September.

Getting There

Hawke's Bay is connected to points north by SH2 to Gisborne and the East Coast, west by SH5 to Taupo and south to Wellington by SH2. The Wairarapa's **arterial road** is SH2. It crosses the Rimutaka Range after Featherston, and descends into the Upper Hutt Valley and Wellington. Highways have light traffic flows, except SH1 along the Kapiti Coast, which is often congested.

Getting Around

InterCity, Newman's and Tranzit Coachlines' **coaches** serve the area. Napier-Hastings and Palmerston North are linked to Auckland and Wellington by regular **air services**, and Freedom Air has flights to Sydney and Brisbane from Palmerston North. **Car rentals** are available at Napier and Palmerston North airports. The **Tranz Metro rail excursion** (Wellington to Masterton in the Wairarapa via the Rimutaka Tunnel) is good, with coach connections from Featherston to Martinborough along the way.

Where to Stay

Hawke's Bay, Wairarapa and the Manawatu have exclusive country retreats, country cottages, historic hotels, guest houses, bed and breakfasts, motor lodges, homestays and farmstays. Rural, country-style accommodation abounds.

Hawke's Bay

Luxury

Hawthorne Country House, Hastings, tel/fax: (06) 878 0035, e-mail: hawthorne@xtra.co.nz web: www.hawthorne.co.nz Classic Hawke's Bay homestead, in the heart of the wine country.

Mangapapa Lodge, Havelock North, tel: (06) 878 3234, fax: (06) 878 1214, reservations: 0800 626 427, e-mail: mangapapa.lodge@xtra.co.nz web: www.mangapapa.co.nz An exclusive, semi-rural retreat east of Hastings.

Mid-range

The County Hotel, 12 Browning St, Napier, tel: (06) 835 7800, fax: (06) 835 7797, reservations: 0800 843 468, e-mail: aspell@xtra.co.nz web: www.countyhotel.co.nz A restored Edwardian building in the heart of the city.

Manawatu

Mid-range

The Coachman Hotel, 134 Fitzherbert Ave, Palmerston North, tel: (06) 356 5065, fax: (06) 356 6692. Hotel-motel on one of the city's major thoroughfares with pool and gym.

The Wairarapa

Luxury

Wharekauhau Country Estate, tel: (06) 307 7581, fax: (06) 307 7799, e-mail: wharekauhau.lodge@xtra.co.nz web: www.wharekauhau.co.nz In a beautiful, remote setting overlooking Palliser Bay.

Martinborough Hotel, town square, tel: (06) 306 9350, fax: (06) 306 9345, e-mail: martinborough.hotel@xtra.co.nz web: www.martinborough-hotel.co.nz A restored colonial hotel.

The Kapiti Coast

Mid-range

Lindale Lodge Motel & Conference Centre, SH1, Paraparaumu North, tel: (04) 298 7933, fax: (04) 297 2544. Close to main shopping area.

Wellington

Luxury

Duxton Hotel, 148–176 Wakefield St, tel: (04) 473 3900, reservations: 0800 655 555, e-mail: res@wellington.duxton.co.nz web: www.duxton.com Opposite Te Papa and Michael Fowler Centre; views of inner city and harbour.

Mid-range

Kingsgate Hotel Oriental Bay, Oriental Parade, tel: 0800 782 548, web: www.kingsgatehotels.co.nz Located on lovely Oriental Bay; harbour views; minutes from beach, cafés, restaurants, theatres and shops.

The Lower North Island at a Glance

Quest on the Terrace, 120 The Terrace, reservations: 0800 508 020, web: www.wellingtonaccom.co.nz Apartments with self-catering facilities, above the central business area; easy access to Lambton Quay's shops and offices.

Where to Eat

The cafés of Courtenay Place are numerous and diverse. The listed hotels also have full dining facilities.

Tours and Excursions

In **Hawke's Bay** are: **Gannet Beach Adventures**, Te Awanga, Hawke's Bay, tel: (06) 875 0898, fax: (06) 875 0849, e-mail: gannetbeach@xtra.co.nz web: www.gannets.com
Bay Tours & Charters, tel: (06) 843 6953, fax: (06) 843 2046, e-mail: info@baytours.co.nz web: www.baytours.co.nz
Dynamic Tours Ltd, tel: (04) 801 6900, fax: (04) 801 6896, e-mail: TheTeam@dynamic-tours.co.nz personalized tours of the Wairarapa.
In **Wellington**, **Hammonds Wellington Scenic Tours** of the Capital City and Coastline, the Kapiti Gold Coast and the Wairarapa, and Palliser Bay, depart daily at 10:00 and 14:00; tel: (04) 472 0869, fax: (04) 471 1730, e-mail: info@wellingtonSightseeingTours.com web: www.WellingtonSightseeingTours.com
Karori Wildlife Sanctuary Tour, Visitor Centre, 41 Waiapu Road (first left after Karori tunnel). Experience first-hand New Zealand's natural heritage, only minutes from the central city. Walk along bush tracks, beside lakes, and witness the progress made in restoring the area's natural wildlife habitat. Guided tours; tel: (04) 920 9200, fax: (04) 920 9000, web: www.sanctuary.org.nz
Somes Island, in the middle of Wellington Harbour, has been a fortification, a quarantine station and a wartime internment island. Public access has been restored and it is now a sanctuary for native plants and birds. Ferries leave from Queens Wharf in the city and Days Bay Wharf in Eastbourne.
Otari Wilton's Bush Native Botanic Garden and Forest Reserve, Wilton Rd, Wilton, is an oasis of native bush and plants, amid the suburbs of Wellington. A canopy walkway takes visitors across a deep gully among the trees. Guided walks every hour on the hour from 10:00–14:00, from the reserve's information centre.
Tours of Parliament , tel: (04) 471 9503, fax: (04) 470 6743; offers guided tours of New Zealand's Parliament in Moleworth St, Thorndon. One-hour tour includes Parliament's history, artworks and architecture. Monday–Saturday 10:00–16:00, Sunday 13:00–15:00.

Useful Contacts

Hawke's Bay visitor information can be obtained from **Hawke's Bay Tourism**, tel: (06) 834 1918, fax: (06) 834 0299, e-mail: hbt@hwakesbaytourism.co.nz web: www.hawkesbaytourism.co.nz
Wairarapa Tourism's head office is in Queen Elizabeth Park, 5 Dixon St, PO Box 814, Masterton, tel: (06) 378 7373, fax: (06) 378 7042, e-mail: tourwai@xtra.co.nz web: www.wairarapanz.com
Destination Manawatu, PO Box 474, Palmerston North, tel: (06) 358 5003, fax: (06) 356 9841, e-mail: dest-man@manawatu.gen.nz
Wellington City Visitor Centre, cnr Wakefield Street and Civic Square, tel: (04) 802 4860, fax: (04) 802 4863, e-mail: Bookings@WellingtonNZ.com web: www.WellingtonNZ.com

NAPIER	J	F	M	A	M	J	J	A	S	O	N	D
AVE. MAX TEMP. °C	24	24	23	20	17	14	14	15	17	19	21	23
AVE. MAX. TEMP. °F	75	75	73	68	63	57	57	59	63	66	70	73
AVE. MIN TEMP. °C	14	14	13	10	7	5	4	5	7	9	11	13
AVE. MIN TEMP. °F	57	57	55	50	44	41	40	41	44	48	52	55
AVE. RAINFALL mm	74	76	74	76	89	86	102	84	56	56	61	58
AVE. RAINFALL in	2.9	3.0	2.9	3.0	3.4	3.3	4.0	3.3	2.2	2.2	2.4	2.3

5
The Upper South Island

The north of the South Island is one of New Zealand's most beautiful regions, offering a variety of attractions: alpine **lakes** and golden **beaches**, vineyards and **wineries**, bush tracks and wilderness **reserves**, all within a relatively small area. The often turbulent **Cook Strait**, separating the North and South Islands, can be crossed by vehicular and passenger ferry, or by air. Regular ferry services connect Wellington with Picton, in the **Marlborough Sounds**, and there are air links from Wellington to Picton, Blenheim and Nelson, the three main towns serving the northern part of the South Island. All inter-island ferries, including the summer-only fast ferries, leave from Wellington's Inter-island Terminal at the northern end of Aotea Quay. As the boat passes from Cook Strait into Tory Channel after its three-hour voyage, there is a sudden contrast between the waters of the strait and those of the Sounds. Crossing the strait by air takes about twenty minutes. On a clear day the flight affords beguiling views of the Sounds' pattern of islands, peninsulas and waterways.

Don't Miss

***** The Marlborough Sounds:** peninsulas, waterways, islands, beaches, bays.
***** Nelson:** a small city with a strong artisan tradition and a fertile hinterland where fine food and wine are produced.
***** Farewell Spit:** sand spit enclosing a bay, a haven for wading and migratory birds.
***** The Kaikoura Coast:** a unique marine environment brings whales, seals and seabirds close to shore.
***** Abel Tasman National Park:** an area of ranges, native forest, streams, rivers and a sheltered coastline.

The Marlborough Sounds

A fretwork of peninsulas, inlets, bays and islands, the Marlborough Sounds rise steeply from the sea, providing a complex of sheltered, picturesque **waterways** which are ideal for boating holidays. This is one region of New Zealand where the boat supersedes the motor vehicle, as many of the sounds are accessible only from the sea. For many local farmers and fishermen the waterways of the Sounds are still their primary conduits of communication.

Opposite: *The coastline near Kaikoura, the South Island's Marinewatch town.*

> **MAPUA**
>
> Mapua coastal village and historic wharf, 30 minutes' drive west of Nelson, is a delightful cluster of art galleries, craft shops, boutiques, cafes and restaurants located beside a tranquil estuary and harbour. Several of the buildings were formerly packing sheds where fruit – mainly apples – was stored before being shipped to Nelson for export.

Capital town of the Sounds is **Picton** (population 4500), at the head of Queen Charlotte Sound. A former whaling station, Picton is today a holiday town and the South Island's railhead. The Community Museum, on the waterfront, displays relics from the whaling era. You can take a number of **cruises** from Picton – the best way to enjoy the beauty and tranquillity of the Marlborough Sounds. The road east of Picton passes Whatamango Bay and the township of Waikawa before it rises to a hill overlooking Port Underwood, a centre for mussel farming.

The Sounds can also be explored by hired **sea kayak** (guided or unguided), or by the **Queen Charlotte Walkway**, a 3-5 day journey between Anakiwa, west of Picton, and Ship Cove, James Cook's main base during his three voyages to New Zealand. The walkway has encompassing views of the sea and the Sounds. There are water taxi connections with either end of the track, or points in between.

Havelock, a small town 28km (17 miles) west of Picton and situated on much-indented **Pelorus Sound**, is another useful base for exploring the region's waterways. This can be done either from the water, including the 'mailboat run' which serves the isolated farms of the Pelorus Sound, or by a number of walking tracks, such as the 20km (12.5-mile) Nydia Walkway, which passes across the area north of Havelock to Duncan Bay, at the head of Tennyson Inlet, deep in the heart of the western Sounds.

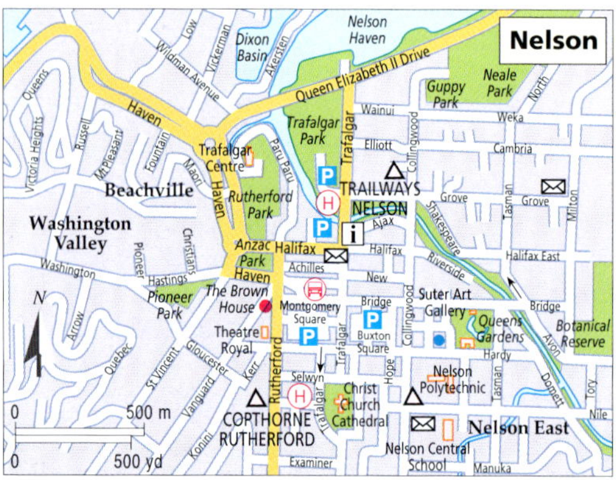

NELSON

The urban centre of the northern region of the South Island and the geographic centre of New Zealand is Nelson (population 43,500), an attractive city on the eastern shore of Tasman Bay. Noted mainly for its scenic setting and Mediterranean climate, Nelson is located in what is one of New Zealand's consistently most sunny districts. In addition, the town boasts an interesting history as well as a present that is rich in artistic activities, in particular pottery and ceramics. Its place names are redolent with the town's thoroughly **English** foundation – Trafalgar Street, Shakespeare Walk, Sussex Street and Hathaway Court, to name but a few – while its central streets are overlooked by the greystone Anglican Christ Church Cathedral.

Above: *Outdoor café dining in sunny Trafalgar Street, Nelson.*

Opposite: *Picton Harbour and its holiday township, Marlborough Sounds.*

As well as being a popular holiday centre, Nelson also has a busy **port** and a fertile hinterland where crops of fruit and vegetables thrive. The combination of alluvial soils, abundant sunshine and natural spring water is the basis of thriving local wine-making and brewing industries. Nelson's satellite town of **Richmond** (population 11,000), situated 14km (8.5 miles) to the southwest, is the gateway to the beautiful rural and coastal districts further west, such as Mapua, Motueka, Abel Tasman National Park and Golden Bay.

The World of Wearable Art and Collectable Cars Museum ***

Ten minutes' drive from Nelson city, the museum holds a fascinating mixture of costumes from past Wearable Art Awards, the internationally acclaimed pageant which began in Nelson, and beautifully restored vintage cars. There is also an art gallery, shop and café. 95 Quarantine Road, Annesbrook, Nelson, tel: (03) 547 4573; e-mail info@wowcars.co.nz web: www.wowcars.co.nz

The Saturday Market **

From early morning to early afternoon every Saturday, the Montgomery Square car park is transformed into a bustling market crammed with stalls selling the goods Nelson is most noted for, namely art and craft work, fresh organic produce, takeaway foods, designer wear and knick-knacks of every description.

Nelson Lakes National Park

South of Nelson, on SH6, are two glacial lakes, Rotoroa and Rotoiti, and the town of St Arnaud on the shores of Lake Rotoiti. Surrounded by forest and mountains, the district offers tramping in summer and skiing June–October, while Lake Rotoiti is popular for its trout fishing, kayaking and sailing. The park's beech forest is rich in native birdlife, including kaka, bellbirds and tuis. Driving east on SH63 takes you to the Wairau Valley, Blenheim and the Marlborough lowlands.

Tasman Bay Coast

SH60 turns northwest from Richmond and passes alongside Tasman Bay on its way to Motueka. The road passes through the **fruit-producing** districts of Appleby, Mapua and Tasman. These settlements are a blend of traditional utilitarian architecture, such as wooden packing sheds, and avant-garde buildings, some of which function as art galleries and cafés. The special nature of the district, with its mountains, rivers, bush and beaches, has attracted many **artists** who live and work here. An inland road, the **Moutere Highway**, winds through pine forests, vineyards and orchards. **Motueka** (population 12,000) itself is a good base for exploring while nearby Kaiteriteri beach is considered one of New Zealand's loveliest.

The **Abel Tasman National Park** is a coastal haven for native flora as well as bird and marine life. At 22,350ha (55,204acres) the smallest of New Zealand's national parks, its conjunction of **land- and seascapes** makes it environmentally unique as well. The coastline consists of golden sand beaches, crystal-clear water and bush-clad headlands. Inland, tracks lead through virgin forest to secluded valleys and mountains over one thousand metres high.

The coast can be explored either by a leisurely, 3–5 day walk along the **Abel Tasman Coastal Track**, or by sea kayak, a launch trip or water taxi ride. In this way the coast and its creatures – seals, dolphins, penguins and other seabirds – can be observed at close quarters. The **inland area** of the park can be reached by road, or it is possible to fly to one of the lodges in the interior. There are several huts in the heart of the park, providing accommodation for hikers.

A Tragic Encounter

On 18 December 1642, **Abel Tasman** anchored his ship, *Heemskerck*, in the large bay enclosed by Farewell Spit. Local Maori warriors went out in canoes to investigate the outlandish newcomers. A violent clash ensued, with fatalities on both sides, and Tasman sailed away without one member of his party setting foot on the new land. The place of anchorage was named Murderers' Bay. Many years later it was renamed, much more aptly, **Golden Bay**. The land south of the bay bears the name **Abel Tasman National Park**.

Golden Bay

Farewell Spit, a sickle of sand forming the northwestern extremity of the South Island, encloses **Golden Bay**, the place where the first European contact was made with Maori, in 1642. The pretty town of **Takaka** (population 1100) lies at the southern end of the bay, and provides rural services as well as visitor information and outlets for the work of local artisans. **Collingwood**, a small beachside settlement a little further along the coast, makes an ideal springboard for exploring Farewell Spit.

Farewell Spit, a bird sanctuary and wetland of international significance, is 25km (15.5 miles) long. It is possible to walk along the base of the spit, or take part in 4WD 'safaris' along it to the lighthouses at **Cape Farewell** and Bush End Point, viewing the **bird habitats** along the way. Species making their home on the spit include migratory wading birds the godwit, wrybill and long-billed curlew, as well as breeding colonies of banded dotterels, royal spoonbills, Caspian terns, wekas and skuas. The western side of the spit is exposed and wild, its sandscapes sculpted by the prevailing southwesterly winds.

South of Golden Bay is **Kahurangi National Park**, approximately 452,000ha (1,116,892 acres) of glaciated mountain ranges and native forest, home to a variety of native flora and fauna. The most notable trail in this region is the **Heaphy Track**, a 4–5 day hike through wonderfully varied landscapes from the Aorere Valley to the mouth of the Kohaihai River, near Karamea.

MARLBOROUGH'S FOOD AND WINE FESTIVAL

A celebration of the Marlborough region's production of fine food and wine takes place on the second Saturday of every February, the largest of its kind in the country. The festival occurs in a field just outside Blenheim, and thousands descend on the district to sample its best vintages and gourmet food. There are exhibitions, arts and crafts displays, live music, as well as the food and drink to enjoy.

Opposite: *Visitors boarding a cruise boat from a beach in Abel Tasman National Park.*
Below: *A gannet colony at Farewell Spit.*

THE MARLBOROUGH PLAINS

The Wairau River and its tributaries have created a fertile valley and plain which today comprises New Zealand's largest **grape-growing region**. The land was first planted extensively in vines during the 1970s, and now, with its fertile alluvial soils and sun-drenched climate (over 2400 sunshine hours per year) the Marlborough region produces more wine than any other area in New Zealand. The Wairau River flows eastward and debouches into Cloudy Bay, near the region's main town, **Blenheim**. Marlborough is also famed for its fine foods, including olives, farmed salmon and mussels, so that gourmet travellers are particularly well catered for here.

From Exploitation to Protection

During the 19th and first half of the 20th century, **whales** were chased and slaughtered in their thousands for the oil their blubber contained. **Whaling stations** were found from the far south to the Hauraki Gulf. **Seals** had also been hunted for their skins from the first years of European settlement. By the mid-20th century, most species of whale were on the brink of extinction.

Today, all whale and seal species are strictly protected and their numbers have recovered. There are thriving **seal colonies** on many parts of the New Zealand coastline, and at Kaikoura you can swim alongside these appealing creatures and also observe whales frolicking in their natural environment. The dignity and size of these marvellous mammals never fails to move those who observe them.

Most of Marlborough's **wineries** are west of Blenheim, close to the main road, SH6, and provide tastings, cellar-door sales and overseas shipping. The principal variety here is Sauvignon Blanc, but Methode Champenoise and Chardonnays also enjoy an excellent reputation. The best-known of the local labels are Cloudy Bay, Stoneleigh, Montana, Lawson's Dry Hills and Daniel Le Brun.

Blenheim (population 21,000) is a town which serves the agricultural districts of the Wairau Valley. Its focus is Seymour Square, an attractive park and garden in the centre of town. Blenheim and its surroundings have a variety of hotels, motels, backpackers' hostels and homestays.

Kaikoura – Marinewatch Town

The seaside settlement of Kaikoura (population 3200), on SH1 midway between Picton and Christchurch, is on a **peninsula** overlooked by the towering **Seaward Kaikoura Range**, a spur of the Southern Alps. In few other areas of New Zealand are snow-capped mountains and deep ocean found in such close proximity. The Pacific Ocean waters just off the town are famous for their rich **marine life**, and visitors descend on Kaikoura throughout the year to watch whales, and swim with seals and dolphins which are readily observable around the peninsula.

The waters off the Kaikoura Peninsula are unusually **deep**, and in the deep canyons on the ocean floor the very cold waters from Antarctica mix with warm waters from the north and east, creating a **rich food chain** for fish, marine mammals and seabirds. 'Kaikoura' means 'crayfish food', a tribute by early Maori to the abundance of crustaceans in the area. Archeological findings have shown that moa-hunting Maori inhabited

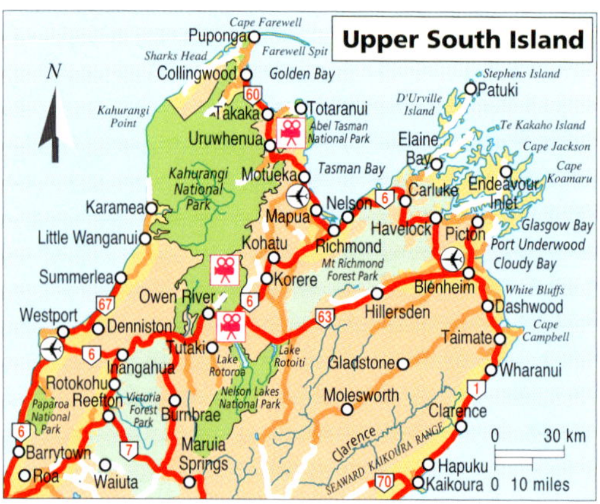

the peninsula 900 years ago. **Maori Leap Cave**, some 2km (1.2 miles) south of Kaikoura on SH1, contains spectacular limestone formations, including stalagmites, stalactites and stone 'straws'.

In the 19th century **whales** were hunted and harpooned off the Kaikoura coast; today these majestic mammals are sought for entirely different reasons. **Giant sperm whales** can be watched at close quarters from purpose-built vessels as they broach and frolic just off the coast. **Dusky dolphins** (one of the most playful and acrobatic of all dolphins) and **fur seals** can be observed or swum alongside. The seals, like the dolphins, can be very responsive to human company. There are several fur seal colonies in the vicinity. **Sharks** can be viewed from the safety of a shark-proof cage. The area also boasts the largest number of pelagic **bird species** within such a small area of New Zealand coastline. It is possible to observe closely some of these birds, including terns, albatross, gannets, shearwaters and mollymawks.

Above: *A broaching whale off the Kaikoura coast is an awesome sight.*

Kaikoura town caters specifically to visitors, with a wide range of accommodation as well as cafés and restaurants specializing in **fresh fish and crayfish**. During the first weekend of October the richness of the local ocean is celebrated at the **Kaikoura Seafest**. A vineyard and winery, the Kaikoura Wine Company, is located high on a limestone bluff just south of the town, on SH1. From the winery's bar and café are magnificent views of the Pacific Ocean and coastline. In the town's hinterland a wide range of **outdoor pursuits** is available, including rafting, horse trekking, 4-wheel motorbiking, tramping and climbing. The mountains and marine life can also be viewed from a light plane. The area is also home to numerous **arts and craftspeople**, whose wares are offered for sale in the town.

Walking the Peninsula

The Kaikoura Peninsula is composed of limestone and siltstone, raised from the sea bed millions of years ago by tectonic forces. An 11km (6.8-mile) walkway follows the shoreline of the peninsula's extremity, from Fyffe House, Kaikoura's oldest building, to Point Kean and around to South Bay. Along the way there are views of sea caves, oyster catchers, shags, and a gull and a seal colony.

The Upper South Island at a Glance

Best Times To Visit

This is New Zealand's sunniest region, its **summer** extending from December–April. The Kaikoura coast is wetter. The busiest time for local holiday-makers is from Christmas to the end of January, so for those seeking to escape the crowds, early December, then February and March are the best times to visit, when the days are hot and dry.

Getting There

Nelson City Airport has regular flights to Auckland, Wellington and Christchurch, and **Blenheim Airport**, 10 minutes west of the town, has daily flights to Auckland, Wellington and Christchurch. **Picton** is the South Island terminal for both traditional and fast **ferries**. There is also a daily return **Tranz Scenic rail service** between Picton and Christchurch, known as The Coastal Pacific route.

Several **coach** lines serve the Nelson-Marlborough region, connecting with Christchurch via Kaikoura or the Lewis Pass.

Getting Around

A number of local operators provide **scenic charters**, **garden tours** and **wine tours**. In **Nelson**, the terminal of **Nelson Coaches**, which provides coach services to Abel Tasman National Park, other New Zealand centres and group charters, is at 27 Bridge Street, tel: (03) 548 0285, e-mail: travel@nelsoncoaches.co.nz web: www.nelsoncoaches.co.nz

DeLuxe Travel Line, Blenheim, provide transport, tours and wine trips in the Marlborough region, tel: (03) 578 5467.

Where to Stay

Many of the best places to stay are at the sea or near it. Many country lodges incorporate restaurants showcasing the area's food, fruit and wines.

Picton-Queen Charlotte Sound

Luxury

Lochmara Lodge, Lochmara Bay, Queen Charlotte Sound, PO Box 172, Picton, tel/fax: (03) 573 4554, e-mail: lochmaralodge@xtra.co.nz web: www.lochmaralodge.co.nz Set on the water, with access to the Queen Charlotte Track.

The Portage Resort Hotel, Kenepuru Road, Marlborough Sounds, tel: (03) 573 4309, fax: (03) 573 4362, e-mail: enquiries@marlboroughnz.co.nz web: www.portage.co.nz Fully refurbished;magical views of the Marborough Sounds.

Nelson

Mid-range

Copthorne Rutherford, Trafalgar Square, tel: (03) 548 2299, fax: (03) 546 3003, e-mail: enquiries@rutherfordhotel.co.nz web: rutherfordhotel.co.nz Central location, 115 rooms.

Wakefield Quay House, 385 Wakefield Quay, Port Hills, Nelson, tel: (03) 546 7275; e-mail: wakefieldquay@xtra.co.nz web: www.wakefieldquay.co.nz Restored colonial villa with glorious harbour views.

Blenheim

Mid-range

Chateau Marlborough, cnr High and Henry streets, PO Box 921, Blenheim, tel: (03) 578 0064, fax: (03) 578 2661, reservations: 0800 75 22 75, e-mail: chateau@marlboroughnz.co.nz web: www.marlboroughnz.co.nz In the heart of town, views of Seymour Square floral gardens.

Kaikoura

Mid-range

The Old Convent, Mt Fyffe Rd, Kaikoura, tel: (03) 319 6603, fax: (03) 319 6690, e-mail: o.convent@xtra.co.nz web: www.theoldconvent.co.nz A preserved homestead, set amid farmland and featuring French cuisine.

Where to Eat

This is known as New Zealand's gourmet region, with seafood, fruit and local wines a speciality. Nelson and Marlborough have everything: fully licensed restaurants, taverns providing bistro meals, rural cafés and wineries.

The Upper South Island at a Glance

Havelock

Mid-range

The Mussel Boys Restaurant, 73 Main Rd, Havelock, tel: (03) 574 2824, fax: (03) 574 2878, e-mail: musselboys@xtra.co.nz web: www.musselboys.co.nz This restaurant specializes in locally farmed mussels.

Nelson

Mid-range

Morrison Street Café, 244 Hardy St, tel: (03) 548 8110, fax: (03) 548 8271, e-mail: morrison.street.café@xtra.co.nz A café-gallery in a historic building. Features local art.

Ma Fish restaurant and bar, 322 Wakefield Quay, Nelson, tel: (03) 539 1307, e-mail: mf@nelsonwaterfront.co.nz web: www.nelsonwaterfront.co.nz Family dining with great harbour views; above the Nelson Yacht Club.

Blenheim

Mid-range

La Veranda Vineyard Café & Restaurant, Domaine Georges Michel Winery, Vintage Lane, tel: (03) 572 9177, fax: (03) 572 7231, e-mail: georgesmichel@xtra.co.nz Dine in a vineyard setting, with views of the Richmond Range.

Kaikoura

Mid-range

FINZ of South Bay, 103 South Bay Parade, Kaikoura, tel: (03) 319 6688, fax: (03) 319 6687, e-mail: finz@xtra.co.nz A quality, intimate seafood restaurant and bar, with a stunning outlook of ocean, mountains and setting sun.

Tours and Excursions

In **Marlborough Sounds** is **The Cougar Line**, The Waterfront, Picton, tel: 0800 50 40 90, fax: (03) 573 7926, e-mail: cougar@voyager.co.nz web: www.cougarlinecruises.co.nz Catamarans tour the sounds, and take walkers and bikers to the Queen Charlotte Track.

Bay Tours Nelson, 48 Brougham St, Nelson, tel: (03) 545 7114, freephone 0800 229 868, fax: (03) 545 7119, e-mail: info@BayToursNelson.co.nz web: http://BayToursNelson.co.nz Wine, craft and scenic tours of the Nelson area.

Abel Tasman National Park Experiences, 265 High St, Motueka, tel: (03) 528 7801, fax: (03) 528 6087, freephone: 0800 223 582, e-mail: info@abeltasman.co.nz web: www.AbelTasman.co.nz Bush walks, launch cruises, water taxis and kayaking.

In **Golden Bay**, contact **Farewell Spit Tours**, Tasman Street, Collingwood, Golden Bay, tel: (03) 524 8257, fax: (03) 524 8939, e-mail: enquiries@FarewellSpit.co.nz web: www.FarewellSpit.com See the spit and bird sanctuary during a leisurely 4WD safari.

Whale Watch Kaikoura, tel: (03) 319 6767, fax: (03) 319 6545, e-mail: res@whalewatch.co.nz web: www.whalewatch.co.nz See the world of nature's leviathan, the Giant Sperm Whale.

Useful Contacts

Destination Marlborough, PO Box 29, Blenheim, tel: (03) 577 5523, fax: (03) 577 5530, e-mail: admin@destinationmarlborough.com web: www.destinationmarlborough.com

Nelson Visitor Information Centre, cnr Trafalgar and Halifax streets, Nelson, tel: (03) 548 2304, fax: (03) 546 7393, e-mail: vin@nelsonnz.com web: www.nelsonNZ.com

Kaikoura Visitor Centre, West End, tel: (03) 319 5641, fax: (03) 319 6819, e-mail: info@kaikoura.co.nz web: www.kaikoura.co.nz

NELSON	J	F	M	A	M	J	J	A	S	O	N	D
AVE. TEMP. °C	18	18	16	13	10	7	7	8	10	12	14	16
AVE. TEMP. °F	64	64	61	55	50	45	45	46	50	54	57	61
AVE. RAINFALL mm	70	70	85	90	105	85	95	98	88	85	70	70
AVE. RAINFALL in	2.7	2.7	3.3	3.5	4.0	3.3	3.7	3.8	3.4	3.3	2.7	2.7

CITY LOOP
YELLOWGLEN Wines
152
TRAMWAYS.

6
Christchurch and the Canterbury Region

The South Island's largest city, **Christchurch** (population 334,107) lies on the eastern edge of the **Canterbury Plains**, New Zealand's largest lowland. The plains were built up over millions of years from silt carried by several large 'braided' **rivers** such as the Waimakariri, the Rakaia and the Rangitata, which emerge from the Southern Alps on the western edge of the plains. Gradually extending eastward, the plains eventually joined **Banks Peninsula**, an extinct volcano indented by several bays and harbours.

Christchurch and Surrounds

Christchurch lies west of Banks Peninsula and spreads northeast to the coast at New Brighton and southeast to the Port Hills and the suburbs of Cashmere and Heathcote. Founded in the 1850s and planned as an antipodean outpost of the Church of England, its central streets were laid out in a **grid pattern**, with the central focus being **Cathedral Square** and the cathedral itself, which was modelled on Caen Cathedral in Normandy. Around this central area are many **neo-Gothic buildings**, and the **River Avon,** with its willow-lined banks, meanders through the city with its delightful **parks and gardens**.

In recent years there has also been a strong growth of **cafés, bars and restaurants** which, along with a **casino**, have enlivened the social and night life of the city. The **Arts Centre**, the **Canterbury Museum** and **Robert McDougall Art Gallery**, on the western fringe of the central city, are all splendid examples of neo-Gothic architecture, as well as centres of cultural heritage.

Don't Miss

*** **The Arts Centre:** a lively arts and craft market and café centre.
*** **Hagley Park:** a 200ha (494-acre) park near the central city, through which the Avon River flows.
*** **Antarctic Centre:** experience the 'Frozen Continent' through sound, light and audio-visual displays.
** **Sumner Beach:** a popular beach east of Christchurch, with a good shopping centre.
** **Hanmer Springs:** a spa town in North Canterbury with a ski-field nearby.

Opposite: *The City Loop tram, a familiar sight in central Christchurch.*

Bringing Back the Tram

Electric trams were the most common form of public transport in New Zealand cities until the 1960s, when they were scrapped in favour of buses. In 1995 **Christchurch** reinstated tram transport, albeit on a limited basis. A **vintage tram** takes passengers on a 'City Loop' from Cathedral Square, down Worcester Street, past the Arts Centre and back to the Square via Rolleston Avenue and Armagh Street. During this nostalgic journey many of central Christchurch's most distinguished historic buildings can be viewed from tram number 152.

The Arts Centre ***

Formerly the University of Canterbury, this complex of Victorian buildings on Worcester Street is now a vibrant arts and craft market and café centre along the street, while inside are quality shops, galleries, a theatre and the **Great Hall**, where lunch-time recitals and performances are held.

Hagley Park ***

This is an expansive park near the central city. Large enough to incorporate a golf course, **Botanic Garden** and sports grounds, it is a delightfully restful area of greenery.

Antarctic Centre ***

A visit to the centre gives you a chance to experience the Antarctica, with which Christchurch has had a connection since the days of **Robert Falcon Scott**. Just five minutes' walk from Christchurch Airport, the centre offers audio-visual displays, as well as sound and light shows.

Lyttelton **

Over the **Port Hills** (or through them, via a road tunnel) is Lyttelton, Christchurch's port. Situated on a crater of an extinct volcano, it is a rather tough port town. **Governors Bay**, at the head of the harbour, is much more genteel, and lies astride the road to **Gebbies Pass** and SH75 and then rises to the crown of Banks Peninsula, providing fine views of the area before descending to Akaroa Harbour. A landmark on SH7 is the Hurunui Hotel (1860), which offers good food and reasonably priced accommodation in a genuine colonial setting.

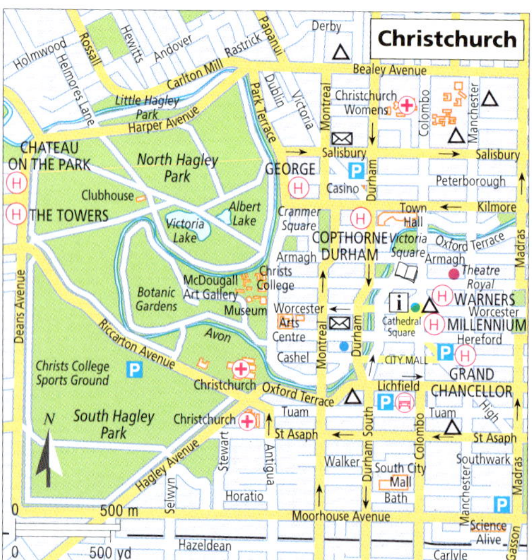

Left: *Akaroa Harbour and its township, situated on Banks Peninsula, an extinct volcano.*

Akaroa Harbour ★★★

Deeper than Lyttelton Harbour, Akaroa Harbour penetrates the peninsula almost to its heart. **Akaroa town**, a lovely holiday town with guesthouses, cafés and art galleries, has a fascinating history. In 1835 a Frenchman, Jean Langlois, saw Banks Peninsula and thought it would be ideal for a French colony. Five years later a shipload of immigrants from France arrived in Akaroa, unaware that the **Treaty of Waitangi** had been signed days earlier, and that New Zealand was now a British colony. Conflict between French and British was avoided by the diplomacy of their officials, the immigrants stayed, and Akaroa developed and maintained a **unique French flavour**.

Today Akaroa perpetuates its 'Frenchness' in its street names (Rue Lavaud, Rue Jolie), colonial architecture, and the **cuisine** in some of its many excellent restaurants. This, combined with its superb setting at the foot of volcanic hills, makes it a place not to be missed. Take a tour on the harbour, or swim with the unique, endangered **Hector's Dolphins**, which make it their home.

The Hurunui

North of Christchurch is the the Hurunui, an area of rolling pastures and downlands. SH1 passes through the **Waipara Valley**, where there are several fine vineyards and wineries, then the SH7 branches west off the main highway. The SH7 runs through the Weka Pass, then alongside the Waiau River before there is a short branch road which leads to the spa village of Hanmer Springs.

The TranzAlpine Express

Considered one of the world's finest **rail journeys**, the TranzAlpine Express excursion departs from Christchurch at 09:00, crosses the **Canterbury Plains**, then travels through **Arthur's Pass National Park**, winding its way through the **Southern Alps** before descending to the town of **Greymouth**, on the West Coast. The journey allows passengers to savour the **natural beauty** and grandeur of the alpine national park – mountains, beech forest and riverbed – from the comfort of a well-appointed railway carriage with large viewing windows and catering services.
The day trip returns to Christchurch at 18:35.

Above: *Visitors enjoying the thermal waters at Hanmer Springs Thermal Reserve in the Hurunui district, North Canterbury.*

Hanmer Springs is at the foot of the Hanmer Range. The tall redwood trees in and around the village, and its mountain backdrop, gives it a North American appearance. Fractured rock provides a path for heated groundwater to flow up the fracture and emerge as hot spring water. **Hanmer Springs Thermal Reserve** is a complex of thermal pools ranging in temperature from 36–42°C (98–108°F). Set in attractive grounds, the pools are relaxing and therapeutic. There are private thermal suites, waterslides and a café providing light lunches and à la carte dining.

From May–October Hanmer Springs is a ski resort. North of the village is the **Hanmer Springs Ski Area**, on the slopes of Mount St Patrick and the St James Ranges. Soaking in a hot pool after a day on the snow is wonderful, and the pools make the ideal après-ski. The town has a range of accommodation, from de luxe to dormitory. Thrillseekers are also catered for: the nearby **Waiau River gorge** offers jet-boating, river rafting, and bungy jumping from the historic Waiau Ferry Bridge.

WALKING BANKS PENINSULA

One of the best ways to experience the rugged beauty of Banks Peninsula is to take the 'four-day, four-night, four-beaches, four-bays' track from and back to **Akaroa**. The 35km (21.7-mile) track goes anti-clockwise around the eastern rim of the extinct volcano, giving **stunning views** of its valleys, bays, sandy beaches, headlands and the Pacific Ocean. Accommodation is provided at comfortable huts and farm houses. Sleeping bags, tramping boots, food, and adequate clothing for all weather, plus a reasonable level of fitness, are the requirements for walkers.

SKIING IN CANTERBURY

Because of the proximity of the Southern Alps, there is a choice of **accessible** and **diverse ski-fields**. There are eight club fields and four commercial ski areas in the region, none more than 90 minutes' drive from snow during the ski season. **Porter Heights** is the closest field to Christchurch.

Mount Hutt, 26km (16 miles) from Methven, is considered one of the finest. With snowmaking technology the area's season lasts from May–November, and it has good skiing and snowboarding conditions. It has a vertical rise of 672m (2204ft) and the longest run is 2km (1.24 miles).

Other club fields in the area are **Craigieburn Valley**, **Mount Olympus**, **Broken River** and **Fox Peak**, in South Canterbury and Mt Lyford Alpine Resort, in North Canterbury. **Erewhon** ski-field, 40km (25 miles) west of Mount Somers, is named after the novel by **Samuel Butler**, who once farmed sheep in the area. 'Erewhon' is (almost) 'nowhere', spelt backwards.

Canterbury Towns

South of Christchurch, SH1 runs through **Rakaia**, **Ashburton** and **Temuka** to **Timaru**. The plains are a broad lowland of pastures and arable crops, rising gently to the foothills of the Southern Alps, which form their backdrop. Viewed from the air they give the appearance of a green, brown and gold patchwork quilt, laced with rivers. One of these, the **Rangitata River**, 22km (13.5 miles) north of Timaru, is renowned for its fine salmon fishing.

Temuka was the home of pioneer aviator and inventor **Richard Pearse**, who some believe achieved powered flight in 1902, months before the Wright brothers flew. There is a **roadside memorial** to his flight, 13km (8 miles) from Temuka, on the road to Waitohi, and information about him in the South Canterbury Museum at Timaru.

Timaru has a busy port and a fine beach, **Caroline Bay**, which is a popular holiday destination. A **piazza** links the central city with the bay and provides views of the Southern Alps, the South Canterbury plains, the port and the Pacific. Three signposted **heritage trails** have been developed in the area to take travellers to the town's most interesting and historic features.

Oamaru, 85km (53 miles) south of Timaru, has many imposing **limestone buildings**, made from locally quarried stone, which give it a more solid appearance than towns where wood is used. The renowned novelist **Janet Frame** (1924–2004) spent some of her life in the town and the Janet Frame Trail takes you past locations which feature in her fiction.

The Jet-boat

Bill (later Sir William) Hamilton was a high country run-holder who in the 1950s, to improve access to his isolated property, invented the jet-boat. This is a highly manoeuvrable craft which planes at high speed in very shallow water, making it ideal on the narrow channels of South Island rivers. Today's jet-boats can achieve speeds of up to 80kph (50mph) and manoeuvre with astonishing ease at high speed. No visit to the South Island is complete without a trip on a jet-boat, which combines thrills with access to some of the high country's most breathtaking scenery.

Christchurch and the Canterbury Region at a Glance

Best Times To Visit

Summer comes early to this area, and temperatures climb from November onwards due to the onset of the 'norwester', a hot, dry Föhn wind from the Southern Alps. Temperatures remain high from January–March, but winters are cold, with snowfalls common on the Port Hills. **Winter** brings fine skiing conditions to the various ski-fields of the region, however, and the season is from June–September.

Getting There

Christchurch International Airport and the domestic terminal are on Memorial Ave, 10km (6 miles) northwest of the city centre. Transport from the airport to the city is readily available by taxi, shuttle, city bus or rental car.

Getting Around

The **Bus Exchange** is located between Colombo and Tuam Streets. A **Big Red Day Pass** gives the visitor a full day's travel on Christchurch bus routes. A single ticket costs NZ$5, a family ticket NZ$10, and tickets are available from the Bus Exchange, any Big Red Bus driver, or the Christchurch Visitor centre, Old Chief Post Office, Cathedral Square West.
Being flat, Christchurch is ideal **bicycle**-riding territory. **City Cycle Hire**, tel: 0800 343 848, will deliver cycles and provide maps.

Where to Stay

Christchurch has a selection of high-quality hotels, motels, guesthouses, bed and breakfast hotels, as well as boutique and lodge accommodation. Many of the hotels are conveniently located, close to the city centre and Hagley Park.

Christchurch

Luxury

Chateau on the Park, 189 Deans Ave, tel: (03) 348 8999, fax: (03) 348 8990, e-mail: res@chateau-park.co.nz web: www.chateau-park.co.nz On the edge of Hagley Park, this hotel has a lovely outlook, five acres of gardens, a pool, restaurants and a cocktail bar.
Hotel Grand Chancellor, 161 Cashel St, tel: (03) 379 2999, fax: (03) 379 0999, reservations: 0800 27 53 37, e-mail: res@grandc.co.nz web: www.grandc.co.nz The city's tallest hotel provides views of Christchurch.
Warners, 50 Cathedral Square, Christchurch, tel: (03) 366 5159, fax: (03) 379 5736, web: www.warnershotel.co.nz Historic hotel in the very heart of the city

Canterbury

Luxury

Bangor Country Inn, Bangor Rd, Darfield, tel: (03) 318 7588, fax: (03) 318 8485, e-mail: sales@bangor.co.nz web: www.bangor.co.nz Set in tranquil English-style parkland, this refurbished country estate has five-star accommodation.
The Heritage Hanmer Springs, 1 Conical Hill Road, Hanmer Springs, tel: (03) 315 7021, fax: (03) 315 7023, e-mail: res.heritagezhp@dynasty.co.nz web: www.heritagehotels.co.nz Set among mature trees and surrounded by hills, the former Hanmer Lodge has been transformed into a luxurious resort while retaining its original Spanish design.

Mid-range

Mulberry House, 9 William St, Akaroa, tel/fax: (03) 304 7778. Restful bed and breakfast, with pool and summer house set among rose gardens.
Oinako Lodge, 99 Beach Rd, Akaroa, tel/fax: (03) 304 8787. A French manor house, built in 1895, only metres from Akaroa Harbour, with balconies and charming gardens.

Where to Eat

Canterbury is fast gaining a reputation as a favourite destination for lovers of fine food. The region, long renowned for its lamb, fresh produce and vintage wines, now features a tantalizing selection of bistros, cafés, restaurants and winery dining.

Christchurch

Luxury

Sign of the Takahe, cnr Dyers Pass and Hackthorne

Christchurch and the Canterbury Region at a Glance

roads, Cashmere Hills, tel: (03) 332 4052, fax: (03) 337 2769. A castle-like Gothic building overlooking the city. Serves morning teas, luncheons and dinners with silver service.
Palazzo del Marinaio, 108 Hereford Street, The Shades Arcade, Christchurch, tel: (03) 365 4640, fax: (03) 365 5911, web: www.palazzo.co.nz A seafood restaurant with dishes prepared the Italian way.

Canterbury

Luxury

C'est La Vie, 33 Rue Lavaud, Akaroa, tel: (03) 304 7314. Fine French cuisine and seafood specialities in an intimate setting, blackboard menu, BYO. Reservations are essential.
The French Farm Winery & Restaurant, French Farm Valley Rd, PO Box 27, Duvauchelle, Akaroa Harbour, tel: (03) 304 5784, fax: (03) 304 5785, web: www.frenchfarm.co.nz Situated in picturesque surroundings, this Provençe-style building houses a spacious restaurant with a summer courtyard.
The Old Post Office Restaurant, 2 Jacks Pass Rd, Hanmer Springs, tel: (03) 315 7461, fax: (03) 315 7246. Fine food and good wine in tasteful, congenial surroundings. Reservations are advisable.

Tours and Excursions

Christchurch Gondola, tel: (03) 384 0700, web: www.gondola.co.nz Breathtaking views of the city, Port Hills and Lyttelton Harbour.
Christchurch Sightseeing (central city sights), bookings: 0800 800 410; departing 09:00, 10:30 and 13:30.
High Country Explorer Tour, reservations: 0800 863 975, web: www.highcountry.co.nz Full-day tour includes coach journey, jet-boat river cruise, 4WD and TranzAlpine rail trip. Tour departs Christchurch city daily at 09:00 in season.
Akaroa French Connection, tel: (03) 366 4556. Bus link between Christchurch and Akaroa and tours of Akaroa and its harbour.
Dolphin Experience Akaroa, 61 Beach Rd, Akaroa, tel/fax: (03) 304 7726. Frolic with the unique **Hector's Dolphins** in Akaroa Harbour, or watch others swimming with them. Tours leave three times a day.
Barry's Bay Traditional Cheese Factory, Main Rd, Barrys Bay, RD Akaroa, tel: (03) 304 5809. See a variety of cheeses made the traditional way, and then purchase the results at very reasonable prices.
The Hanmer Connection, tel: 0800 377 378, offers a daily bus service to the Hanmer Springs Thermal Resort from Christchurch Visitors Centre. Hanmer to Kaikoura return on Tuesdays, Thursdays and Saturdays.
For **jet-boating** and fishing on the Rakaia River, tel: (03) 318 6574. A wonderful opportunity to experience the extreme manoeuvrability and power of the jet-boat, and also see the dramatic Rakaia Gorge and alpine scenery.

Useful Contacts

Christchurch & Canterbury Visitor Centre, Old Chief Post Office, Cathedral Square West, tel: (03) 379 9629, fax: (03) 377 2424, e-mail: info@christchurchnz.net web: www.christchurchnz.net
Akaroa Information Centre, 80 Rue Lavaud, Akaroa, tel/fax: (03) 304 8600, e-mail: akaroa.info@clear.net.nz web: www.akaroa.com
Hurunui Tourism Board, 66 Carters Road, Amberley, tel: (03) 314 8816, fax: (03) 314 9181, e-mail: info@hurunui.com web: www.hurunui.com

CHRISTCHURCH	J	F	M	A	M	J	J	A	S	O	N	D
AVE. TEMP. °C	17	17	16	13	9	7	7	8	10	12	14	16
AVE. TEMP. °F	63	63	61	55	48	45	45	46	50	54	57	61
AVE. RAINFALL mm	56	43	48	48	66	66	69	48	46	43	48	56
AVE. RAINFALL in	2.2	1.6	1.8	1.8	2.5	2.5	2.6	1.8	1.7	1.6	1.8	2.1

7
The Southern Alps and Lakes

The South Island's Alps and alpine lakes are not only New Zealand's most imposing geographical feature, they also provide a superb **recreational region**. The jagged Alps were formed from tectonic uplift due to the 'collision' between the Pacific and the Indo-Australian plates. The plates are pushing hardest against each other in the central part of the Southern Alps, where the two highest mountains are found: **Aoraki Mount Cook** at 3754m (12,313ft), and **Mount Tasman** at 3497m (11,470ft). New Zealanders know the Southern Alps as the 'high country'.

The forces of erosion (water, wind, ice) have sculpted the mountains into distinctive shapes. Sufficiently high in many areas never to lose their snow caps, the Alps were shaped most dramatically by **glaciation** during the Ice Age which began about 2.4 million years ago and ended about 12,000 years ago. During this era the river valleys of the Southern Alps were occupied by mighty glaciers which carved them into **U-shapes** and cut off their tributaries to create 'hanging valleys'.

When the climate became warmer again and the glaciers melted, eroded material carried by the rivers of ice, called **moraine**, was deposited in the valleys. If the moraine blocked a valley, a long deep lake formed behind it. Most of the lakes in the Southern Alps – such as **Te Anau**, **Wakatipu**, **Tekapo** and **Wanaka** – were formed in this way. Shingle-bedded, glacier-fed rivers pour from the Alps, their courses '**braided**' into myriad channels, feeding the lakes and building up alluvial plains from their silt-laden waters.

Don't Miss

*** **Aoraki Mount Cook:** New Zealand's highest point, with the country's largest glacier, the Tasman Glacier.
*** **Arrowtown:** visit the Lakes District Museum for the history of the area.
*** **Queenstown Gardens:** only a few minutes' walk from the town centre.
*** **Lake Wakatipu:** enjoy a cruise across to Walter Peak Station on the coal-fired steamer *TSS Earnslaw*.
*** **Jetboating:** a trip on a jet boat provides a thrilling journey into Queenstown's magnificent hinterlands.

Opposite: *Church of the Good Shepherd, Lake Tekapo, South Island.*

The cool Ice Age climate put New Zealand's flora and fauna under quite extraordinary evolutionary pressure. Some species became extinct, while others evolved new forms to cope with the changes. The **kea** *(Nestor notabilis)*, the only true alpine parrot in the world, developed from ancestors that once inhabited warm lowlands. Today the inquisitive kea, which is a dull green with a crimson abdomen and with orange patches on the underside of its wings, makes both the lowlands and highland forests of the South Island its home. Its cousin, the **kaka** *(N. meridionalis)* inhabits mainly the lowland forest.

Stands of **red beech** *(Northofagus fusca)* and **black beech** *(N. solandri)* thrive in the dry, cool climate of the Southern Alps. The red beech covers the foothills and inland valley floors, while the black beech clothes the high country, covering valleys to the treeline. **Silver beech** *(N. menziesii)* dominates the moister mountains to the west.

Cracks and caves in the mountains are occupied by the alpine **weta** *(Hemideina maori)*, an indigenous insect which, though it looks fearsome, is harmless. More common is the New Zealand **falcon** or bush hawk *(Falco novaeseelandiae)*, which can be seen soaring above the high country. The hawk's food includes rabbits, hares and lizards.

Hundreds of **flowering alpine plants** grow nowhere in the world except New Zealand's Southern Alps. Best known of these is the white-flowered, so-called **Mount Cook lily** *(Ranunculus lyallii)*, which is actually a buttercup – the world's largest. Alpine daisies are conspicuous members of the snow tussock herb-fields. The **snow**

Power from the River

Engineers were quick to appreciate the potential of the South Island's high country and rivers for generating hydro-electricity, in particular the headwater lakes of the 209km (129-mile) **Waitaki River**. Power station construction began in the late 1920s and there are now 12 power stations on the river, providing about one third of New Zealand's power. The main dams are the **Benmore** (which is made of earth) and the **Aviemore**. Viewing areas allow visitors to appreciate the vast scale of construction the building of these dams involved.

tussocks themselves *(Chionochloa)* are slow growing and epitomize the vegetation of the high country, their spiky heads crowning the ranges with gold and russet.

The Southern Alps is a region of overwhelming beauty on a grand scale. Formerly isolated, today the high country can be penetrated and enjoyed with relative ease thanks to helicopters, light aircraft, jet-boats and 4WD vehicles. The national parks, **Arthur's Pass**, **Mount Cook** and **Mount Aspiring**, remain wonderful preserves free of commercial development, but crossed by walking tracks so that their spectacular wildernesses can still be savoured.

Aoraki Mount Cook

Aoraki Mount Cook, at a height of 3754m (12,313ft), is **New Zealand's highest point**, in spite of its summit being reduced by about 10m (33ft) during a landslide in 1991. Two glacial lakes, **Tekapo** and **Pukaki**, lie to the south of Aoraki Mount Cook, and the **Tasman Glacier**, New Zealand's largest at 28km (17 miles) long and 3km (1.8 miles) wide, flows east and feeds Lake Pukaki. To the southeast of the lakes is the distinctive grassland region, the **Mackenzie Basin**, named after a 19th-century sheep-stealer, James Mackenzie.

The waters of river-fed **Lake Tekapo** are a striking **turquoise** shade. This distinctive colour is caused by sunlight reflecting from tiny rock particles ground from the Alps and suspended in the water. Near the outlet of Lake Tekapo is the superbly sited **Church of the Good Shepherd**, built in stone in 1935 to commemorate the Mackenzie Country's pioneers.

The road to **Mount Cook village** and The Hermitage (its main accommodation centre) follows the western shore of Lake Pukaki, and gives striking views of Aoraki Mount Cook. Above the village is the mountain itself, and surrounding the peak is **Mount Cook National Park**, a World Heritage site 700km^2 (434 sq miles) in area. The park has several **tramping tracks** to suit people of all

The Lure of Gold

In May 1861 Gabriel Read, an Australian who had worked in the goldfields of California and Victoria, found gold at Blue Spur, Tuapeka, south of Lawrence in Otago. A rush of immigration followed, mostly from Australia and California, and later some from China. Further and larger discoveries in the Clutha River began another frenzied influx. Towns like Cromwell and Arrowtown mushroomed, and by the late 1860s Dunedin was New Zealand's largest commercial centre. The gold was panned, sluiced and dredged from the riverbeds and terraces, leaving scars on the landscape. From 1857–70, New Zealand exported 5.54 million ounces of gold, 49 per cent of which came from Otago and Southland. Winky's Museum, in the Skippers Canyon near Queenstown, has a gold sluicing 'cannon' where panning for gold can still be done.

Below: *A light sightseeing plane flies above the scenic Southern Alps.*

THE CHINESE SETTLEMENT OF ARROWTOWN

Some of the most poignant relics of Arrowtown's gold mining history are the remains of the houses and shops built in the 1860s by **Chinese miners** beside the Arrow River, on the outskirts of the town. Segregated by European prejudice and cultural differences, the Chinese men built their houses of tin, stone and wood and lived a spartan existence, working over the tailings along the nearby river by day, and at night playing mah-jong, smoking opium and guarding their hard-earned gold. Some returned to China with their savings, others died in Otago, lonely and far from home.

fitness levels, from supremely testing alpine ascents to easy, day-long hikes. Detailed tramping information is available from the Department of Conservation in Mount Cook village. The scenery here is magnificent, and includes alpine peaks, large lakes, tarns, glaciers, waterfalls, streams and rivers. The mighty **Tasman Glacier** and its terminal lake lie 8km (5 miles) northeast of Mount Cook village. Scenic flights in fixed-wing planes and helicopters provide exhilarating views of the Alps and glaciers.

Arrowtown

Probably New Zealand's **prettiest small town**, Arrowtown is a 20-minute drive from Queenstown and nestles under a range of hills beside the peaceful Arrow River. Born of the hectic **gold** rush in the early 1860s, it is today preserved as a 19th-century settlement. Its main street, **Buckingham Street**, is lined with cafés, restaurants, boutiques and mature exotic trees which take on glorious golden shades every April. The shops specialize in New Zealand products, including knitwear and leather garments, greenstone and gold jewellery, arts and crafts.

Surrounding Arrowtown's colonial core are several new housing developments, including the upmarket **Millbrook Resort and Country Club** and golf course. A climb up **Tobin's Track** above the town provides panoramic views of Arrowtown and the picturesque scenery surrounding the town. **The Lakes District Museum** in Buckingham Street, which opens daily, is very good, featuring displays of pioneer days in the Wakatipu basin, along with a small bookshop and exhibition centre. Visitors can try their hand at panning for gold in the river behind the town.

The remains of the gold-mining village of **Macetown**, now a ghost town, lie about 16km (10 miles) away from Arrowtown and can be reached by trekking, mountain biking or four-wheel driving.

Opposite: *The bridge at Skippers Canyon is the departure platform for intrepid bungy jumpers.*
Below: *Stables Restaurant in Arrowtown, one of a number of excellent eateries in the historic township.*

Cromwell and Wanaka

Two roads go to Wanaka from Arrowtown: the shorter, rougher SH89 crosses the **Crown Range**, the longer, sealed SH6 goes via the **Kawarau Gorge**, **Cromwell** and **Lake Dunstan**. The Crown Range road has the advantage of passing through Cardrona, with its restored colonial pub and good ski-field; the Kawarau Road follows the 'wine trail' route to Cromwell.

Cromwell was largely rebuilt during the 1970s, when the **Clutha River** was dammed by the Clyde Dam, creating Lake Dunstan and burying much of the area's history. The drive from Cromwell to Wanaka in the valley of the upper Clutha River goes past **classic Central Otago landscapes**: arid brown hills, tussock and briar vegetation, schist tors, wide basins and fertile valleys. Once ravaged by gold seekers, the region now has fine wool **merino sheep**, farmed **deer**, irrigated **orchards** and **vineyards**. 'Central's' haunting landscapes are captured by the Dunedin-based painter, **Grahame Sydney** and its distinctive human characters inhabit the prose fiction of the acclaimed New Zealand writer, **Owen Marshall**.

Second only to Queenstown as a visitor resort centre, yet with a slower pace, **Wanaka** reposes on the southern shore of **Lake Wanaka**. Here are boating and **water sports** galore, while as the gateway to **Mount Aspiring National Park World Heritage** area, the Wanaka district offers magnificent **mountaineering** and **tramping**. Several outdoor activities can be enjoyed here, including skiing **Treble Cone** field, 20km (12.5 miles) to the west. Wanaka is New Zealand's pre-eminent **vintage plane** centre. Buffs can relish the **New Zealand Fighter Pilots' Museum** and the biennial '**Warbirds over Wanaka**' airshow, held every second Easter. Scenic flights, including a spin in a vintage Tiger Moth, can be taken from Wanaka's **airport**, east of town. The dry, clear skies and scenic beauty of the area are ideal for such joy riding.

A Sporting Nation

The top ten sports and physical activities for New Zealand **women**:
- Gardening – 63 per cent
- Short walks – 45 per cent
- Long walks – 43 per cent
- Exercising at home – 33 per cent
- Swimming – 32 per cent
- Aerobics – 20 per cent
- Exercise classes – 18 per cent
- Cycling – 14 per cent
- Netball – 11 per cent
- Tramping – 10 per cent

The top ten sports and physical activities for New Zealand **men**:
- Gardening – 44 per cent
- Short walks – 29 per cent
- Long walks – 29 per cent
- Swimming – 26 per cent
- Golf – 25 per cent
- Exercising at home – 24 per cent
- Running or jogging – 19 per cent
- Cycling (recreational and competitive) – 18 per cent
- Exercise classes or gym – 16 per cent
- Touch rugby – 14 per cent

Queenstown

New Zealand's premier tourist destination, Queenstown is truly a town for all seasons. Set on the slopes beside **Lake Wakatipu**, the country's third largest, and with glorious views of the lake in several directions, Queenstown is surrounded by mountains. It has cold, dry winters and hot, dry summers. Its stunning scenery is popular for overseas and New Zealand movie makers, notably Peter Jackson with his adaptation of the *Lord of the Rings* trilogy.

Most dramatic of Queenstown's mountains are the aptly-named **Remarkables** at 2343m (7688ft). These saw-toothed ramparts of rock rise sheer from the lake's eastern shore – a hypnotic sight throughout the year: whether white with snow in winter, or during the rest of the year when the bare, craggy face constantly alters its expression with the changing angle of the sun's rays.

More accessible is **Ben Lomond**, the mountain to the west of the town. A **gondola** takes visitors up a precipitous slope to the **Skyline Restaurant**, 762m (2500ft); from its viewing deck are sublime views of Queenstown, Queenstown Hill just behind the town, Wakatipu Lake and its peninsulas, The Remarkables, **Cecil Peak**, and the ski field of **Coronet Peak** at a height of 1646m (5400ft). A walkway continues upwards from the Skyline to Ben Lomond itself, 1747m (5747ft), where there are even grander vistas of both the lake and the surrounding mountains.

Lady of the Lake

Almost inseparable from Lake Wakatipu is *TSS Earnslaw*, the coal-fired vessel which has plied the water since 1912.

Originally serving farmers in remote areas around the lake, today the *Earnslaw* cruises between Queenstown and Walter Peak station.

A trip on the *Earnslaw* is a must. The venerable 'Lady of the Lake' goes back to another era, but has comforts such as onboard bar and café, and a piano on her upper deck.

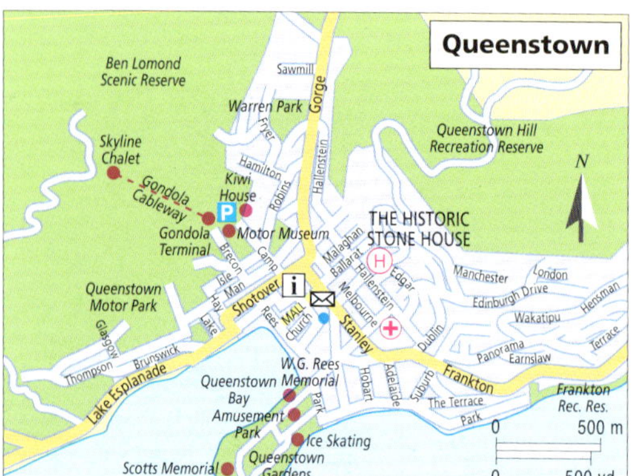

Queenstown is easy to explore. A walkway follows the lake shore, to Frankton Arm in one direction, Sunshine Bay the other. The shore in front of the town – **The Mall** and **Marine Parade** – has a jetty and beach, and there are few better places to be than here with the sun setting over Lake Wakatipu. In midsummer it does not get dark until 22:00. There are a variety of eateries, from fast food franchises to ethnic restaurants, and many souvenir boutiques and gift-shops. The historic Eichardts buildings on the lakefront is now a luxury retail and accommodation complex.

Queenstown's attraction as an outdoor sports destination was based on **skiing** and **mountaineering**; both are still well catered for. The mountains are laced with walkways and there are four ski-fields in the district: **Coronet Peak**, **The Remarkables**, **Cardrona** and **Treble Cone**. To these activities have been added an array of **adventure tourism activities**. You can participate in: bungy jumping, jet-boating, hang-gliding, horse trekking, mountain biking, luge riding, heli-skiing, parasailing, parapenting, sky-diving, rafting, kayaking, river surfing, four-wheel-drive safaris, flying fox riding, hot-air ballooning and jet-skiing.

There are also **more sedate activities**: cruising on the lake, following its shoreline walkways, trout fishing, bus trips, golf and skating. There is an excellent aviary at the foot of the Skyline gondola, where kiwis and other rare native birds can be observed closely in a bush setting.

Central Otago produces quality cool-climate **wines**. Its schisty soils, harsh winters and hot dry summers are ideal for growing grapes, particularly **Pinot Noir**. There are several wineries within a short drive of Queenstown, in the **Wanaka Basin** and the **Kawarau Gorge**. The vineyards of the gorge are beautiful, with rows of vines on the edge of the ravine, and mountains in the background. The wineries have tours, tastings and cellar sales, and some have restaurants.

THE ROUTEBURN TRACK

One of New Zealand's finest **wilderness walks**, the three-day, 39km (24-mile) Routeburn Track, begins near the little lakeside town of **Glenorchy**, a 50-minute drive along the shores of Lake Wakatipu from Queenstown. **Maori** trekked up the Routeburn Valley 500 years ago in search of precious *pounamu* (jade) to make their tools, ornaments and weapons. Today the track crosses the **Humboldt Mountains** and passes some spectacular alpine scenery, including alpine herb fields, beech forests, glaciated slopes, lakes and waterfalls. Several comfortable huts provide accommodation along the way.

Opposite: *Lake Wakatipu reflects the Remarkable Range in its waters.*
Below: *Lake Wakatipu, with Queenstown and Queenstown Hill situated on its shores.*

The Southern Alps and Lakes at a Glance

Best Times To Visit

This region appeals all year. In **summer**, December–March, it is hot and dry, in **autumn** the deciduous trees bring glorious colour, in **winter** the ski slopes are mantled with snow, and in **spring** new growth returns. Most adventure activities the region is renowned for can be enjoyed throughout the year.

Getting There

Queenstown's airport is at **Frankton**, 7km (4.3 miles) northeast of Queenstown. There are flights from here to nearly all the North and South Island centres. **Shuttle buses** run every few minutes from outside the terminal to central Queenstown and **rental cars** and **taxis** are available at the airport. The **Mount Cook Bus** and **InterCity Coachlines Terminal** is in Church St. Daily coach services go to Queenstown from Dunedin, Christchurch and Franz Josef, and **Kiwi Discovery** has a shuttle service between Christchurch and Queenstown on weekdays. Major coachlines run buses to Aoraki Mount Cook from Christchurch via Tekapo, and from Queenstown. **Mount Cook Airport**, 3km (2 miles) south of Mount Cook village, receives regular daily flights.

Getting Around

Central Queenstown is best explored **on foot**. A trip on the **gondola**, from its terminal at the end of Brecon St to the Skyline Restaurant above Queenstown, is exhilarating. There are regular Queenstown to Arrowtown and Queenstown to Wanaka **bus** services, which leave from outside McDonalds in Camp St; several **rental car** companies are in the central town area.

Where to Stay

Mount Cook Village

Mid-range

Hermitage Aoraki Mt Cook, on the northwest edge of Mt Cook village, tel: (03) 435 1809, fax: 435 1879, e-mail: reservations.hermitage@xtra.co.nz web: www.mount-cook.com Includes rooms with balconies, four eateries, plus several chalets and motel units.

Omarama

Mid-range

The Omarama Countrytime Resort Hotel, tel: (03) 438 9894, fax: (03) 438 9791, reservations: 0800 273 767, e-mail: countrytimeresort@xtra.co.nz web: www.resorts.co.nz Well-appointed rooms and self-contained apartments.

Queenstown

Luxury

Millennium Hotel, cnr Frankton Rd and Stanley St, Queenstown, tel: 0800 645 536, e-mail: central.res@mckhotels.co.nz web: www.millenniumqueenstown.co.nz Stylish accommodation, a stroll away from Queenstown Gardens and Lake Wakatipu.

The Historic Stone House, 47 Hallenstein St, tel: (03) 442 9812, fax: (03) 441 8293, e-mail: stone.house@xtra.co.nz web: www.stonehouse.co.nz This bed and breakfast (built in 1874) offers Victorian dignity and modern comforts.

Millbrook Resort, Malaghans Rd, Arrowtown, tel: (03) 441 7000, fax: (03) 442 1145, e-mail: marketing@millbrook.co.nz web: www.millbrook.co.nz Luxury cottage, villa suite and village inn accommodation next to a championship golf course.

Wanaka

Mid-range

Edgewater Resort, Sargood Drive, tel: (03) 443 8311, fax: (03) 443 8323, reservations: 0800 108 311, e-mail: edgewater@xtra.co.nz web: www.edgewater.co.nz Lakefront location, mountain views and sports amenities.

Cardrona Hotel, Cardrona Valley, between Queenstown and Wanaka on SH89 (25km from Wanaka), tel/fax: (03) 443 8153. A historic restored colonial hotel, restaurant, bar and beer garden. A popular watering-hole for skiers.

Where to Eat

No area in New Zealand outside the main cities has as many eateries as this region. There is a huge variety of restaurants, cafés, pubs, brasseries and snack bars, along with the popular fran-

The Southern Alps and Lakes at a Glance

chise food joints in Queenstown. Standards vary greatly, however, from *haute cuisine* to downright awful! The following eateries are recommended.

Queenstown

Mid-range

Boardwalk Seafood Restaurant & Bar, Steamer Wharf, Queenstown, tel: (03) 442 5630, e-mail: dine@boardwalk.net.nz web: www.boardwalk.net.nz On Queenstown Bay's shore; views of Lake Wakatipu and the Remarkable Range.

The Pig and Whistle, Ballarat St, tel: (03) 442 9055. Snacks and light meals, olde English pub ambience; the beer garden is great for people watching.

Gibbston Valley Winery Restaurant, Gibbston RD1, SH6, tel: (03) 442 6910, fax: (03) 442 6909, e-mail: gvwltd@gvwines.co.nz web: www.gibbston-valley-wines.co.nz Courtyard dining beside the winery, in the centre of pinot noir territory, the ruggedly beautiful Kawarau Gorge.

Wanaka

Mid-range

Kai Whakapai Café, Ardmore St, tel: (03) 443 7795. Stylish indoor or outdoor dining, blackboard menu.

Tours and Excursions

Shotover Jet, PO Box 189, Queenstown, tel: 0800 746 868, fax: (03) 442 7467, e-mail: reservations@shotoverjet.co.nz web: www.shotoverjet.com Jet-boat up spectacular Shotover Gorge.

Shotover Canyon Swing, tel: (03) 442 6990, 0800 279 464, e-mail: info@canyonswing.co.nz web: www.canyonswing.co.nz Eight ways to bungy jump or be released, from mild to extreme.

Dart River Safaris, Glenorchy, tel: (03) 442 9992, 0800 327 853, e-mail: reservations@dartriver.co.nz web: www.dartriver.co.nz Combines jet boating with a forest walk and backroad excursion.

Alpine Recreation, PO Box 75, Lake Tekapo, tel: (03) 680 6736, freephone: 0800 006 096, fax: (03) 680 6765, email: climb@alpinerecreation.com web: www.alpinerecreation.com Guided ski touring and snow shoeing across the Mt Cook Range and in the high country above Lake Tekapo.

Queenstown Wine Trail, tel: (03) 442 3799, fax: (03) 442 3796, e-mail: qwinetrail@xtra.co.nz Visit four of the world's southernmost vineyards.

Useful Contacts

Destination Queenstown, P.O.Box 353, Queenstown, tel: (03) 442 7440, fax: (03) 442 7441, e-mail queenstown@xtra.co.nz web: www.queenstown-nz.co.nz

Mount Cook National Park Visitor Centre, combined with the DOC office, located in the Hermitage Hotel buildings and chalets, tel: (03) 435 1186, fax: (03) 435 1080, e-mail: monvin@nzhost.co.nz

Queenstown Visitor Information Network, Clocktower Centre, cnr Shotover / Camp streets, Queenstown, tel: (03) 442 4100, fax: (03) 442 8907, e-mail: qvc@xtra.co.nz

The Station, cnr Camp and Shotover streets, PO Box 1014, Queenstown. For information, bookings and sightseeing, tel: (03) 442 5252, fax: (03) 442 5384, e-mail: info@thestation.co.nz web: www.new-zealand.com/TheStation

Milford Track Guided Walk, PO Box 259, Queenstown, tel: (03) 441 1138, fax: (03) 441 1124, reservations: 0800 659 255, e-mail: mtinfo@milfordtrack.co.nz web: www.new-zealand.com/milfordtrack

Wanaka Visitor Information Centre, Waterfront Log Cabin, Ardmore St, Box 147, Wanaka, tel: (03) 443 1233, fax: (03) 443 1290, e-mail: info@lakewanaka.co.nz web: www.lakewanaka.co.nz

QUEENSTOWN	J	F	M	A	M	J	J	A	S	O	N	D
AVE. TEMP. °C	17	16	14	11	7	5	4	6	9	11	13	15
AVE. TEMP. °F	63	61	57	52	44	32	39	42	48	52	55	59
AVE. RAINFALL mm	79	72	74	72	64	58	59	63	66	77	64	62
AVE. RAINFALL in	3.1	2.8	2.9	2.8	2.5	2.2	2.3	2.4	2.5	3.0	2.5	2.4

8
The Wild West Coast

There is no region in New Zealand quite like the West Coast. Physically **isolated** from the rest of the South Island by the Southern Alps, it is 600km (372 miles) from Karamea in the north to Jackson Bay in the south, but from west to east, from the Tasman Sea to the Alps, the region averages only about 30km (18.5 miles). **Three road passes** through the Alps – the Lewis, Arthur's and Haast – link the West Coast to the rest of the South Island, as does the Otira **rail tunnel**, a key section of the rail link between Greymouth and Christchurch.

The **long, narrow West Coast** is a region of wind-swept beaches, rugged headlands, mighty glaciers, virgin rain forests, lakes and swift-flowing rivers, all overlooked by the Southern Alps and exposed to the prevailing southwest winds. These winds bring **heavy orographic (mountain) rainfall** to the coast. Franz Josef, for example, has a mean annual rainfall of 5092mm (198in). It rains there on an average of 189 days a year.

The only towns of any size, Westport and Greymouth, are in the north, with smaller Hokitika about halfway along the coast. Other settlements are tiny and far apart, and some are true 'ghost towns'. The West Coast's appeal lies in its **unspoilt natural landscapes**.

In the south are Westland and Mount Aspiring national parks, and in the north Paparoa National Park and Victoria Forest Park, all areas of **superb scenic beauty**.

As well as being set apart by nature itself, the West Coast has also long had an **independent** human spirit. 'Coasters' take a lot of pride in the fact that they do

Don't Miss

***** Fox and Franz Josef:** Though global warming has caused the glaciers to 'retreat' during the last century, they are still awe-inspiring. Explore them by taking a guided walk with local operators.
***** Pancake Rocks, Punakaiki:** Erosion has 'stratified' the limestone into layered columns resembling stacks of giant pancakes. The waves have also created blowholes.
***** Shantytown:** A reconstructed 19th-century gold-rush town to the south of Greymouth, consisting of restored colonial buildings.

Opposite: *The rocky shoreline of the Tasman Sea, southern West Coast.*

The Wonderful Whitebait

One of New Zealand's culinary delicacies is the native whitebait, a tiny fish which is caught in nets in the rivers of the West Coast as it migrates seasonally in shoals from the open sea to the upper reaches of the river to mature and spawn. The transparent whitebait, known to Maori as *inanga* and to science as *Galaxias maculatus*, are fished for along the riverbanks during the spring. Once abundant, they are today relatively scarce and command high retail and restaurant prices. They are delectable when made into fritters, fried in butter and served with fresh herbs.

things differently from the rest of New Zealand. This attitude probably derives from a combination of the coast's physical isolation, its strong Irish settlement in colonial times and a persisting pioneer tradition. True 'Coasters' are **mavericks** and proud of the fact.

The coast's economic history began centuries ago. Maori visited the area in search of precious **greenstone** (jade), which was found in the beds of rivers flowing down from the Alps. They called the greenstone *pounamu*. This early exploitation of the coast's resources was minimal, however, compared with what followed after **alluvial gold** was discovered in the rivers and beach sands in 1863. There was a **rush of immigrants** to the coast, the ports of Hokitika and Greymouth were jam-packed with sailing ships, and ramshackle towns sprang up overnight. By 1867 there were 30,000 prospectors on the West Coast goldfields.

The coast's gold output did not match Otago's, but it did not decline as fast either. The alluvial

and beach leads were still workable on a reduced scale by individual miners and small groups after the huge gold rushes had passed. Companies continued mining with large **dredges** until well into the 20th century. Areas of gold workings, such as those at Goldsborough, near Hokitika, can still be visited as historic sites.

Above: *The spectacular Pancake Rocks at Punakaiki, West Coast.*
Opposite: *Visitors can re-enact the gold rush at Shantytown near Greytown, or (pictured here) outside Hokitika.*

Early in the 20th century, mining of the coast's rich **coal** reserves grew to replace gold as its main source of income. By the 1960s, however, seams in some areas had become uneconomic and several coal-mining settlements were completely abandoned. The mining and forestry industries have since declined, leading to a reduction in work opportunities for many West Coasters.

Today the coast's economy is based on **coal-mining**, **cattle-raising**, **fishing**, **forestry** and **tourism**. The West Coast's coal mines still supply one-third of the nation's coal. Exotic trees are a renewable resource, but the milling of slower-growing and more valuable native trees such as rimu and beech has become extremely contentious, with **conservationists** (most of whom do not live on the West Coast) and the timber companies and their employees at loggerheads, so to speak, over the issue.

Tourism has grown enormously, with visitors (particularly backpackers) attracted to the region's forests, lakes and rivers, rip-roaring history, eccentric lifestyles and thriving 'alternative' culture. The appellation '**adventure tourism**' suits the Wild West Coast down to the ground.

Paparoa National Park

One of the smallest and most recently proclaimed of New Zealand's national parks, Paparoa occupies much of the western flank of the mountain range of the same name, just inland from Punakaiki's Pancake Rocks and mid-way between Greymouth and Westport. Rising to a height of more than 1000m (3281ft), the parkland includes many karst or limestone formations such as caves, gorges and sinkholes, which can be observed from its several walking tracks. The shapely nikau palm, the world's most southerly growing palm, is abundant in this area.

Coastal Towns

Westport was born of the gold rush, then sustained by the mining and export of coal. Across the Buller River, Carter's Beach is good for swimming, and a little further along the coast at Tauranga Bay, near Cape Foulwind, there is a seal colony. Inland, just off SH67 to the north of Westport is the

Above: *It is obvious why Lake Matheson, near Fox Glacier, is known as the 'mirror lake'.*

now-derelict settlement of **Denniston**, once a thriving coal-mining town, setting for the bestselling novels *The Denniston Rose* (2003) and its sequel, *Heart of Coal* (2004), by Jenny Pattrick. The main attractions today are its industrial relics, notably the **Denniston Incline** – a haulway which was used to lower the mined coal from bins to the railhead 1500m (4920ft) below. Tours are available to historic and working mining sites. **Coal Town** in Westport displays very realistic exhibits depicting the history of the area.

Greymouth is the coast's largest town. It is another centre which owes its origins to the gold rush days. Some of its 19th-century buildings remain. A visit to the **Jade Boulder Gallery**, where local greenstone is cut and shaped into jewellery, is worthwhile, as is a tour of **Monteith's Brewing Company**, where quality ales and lagers are brewed. History House has a fascinating collection of photographs from Greymouth's past, including those of the floods which affected the town before the construction of a wall to protect it from the Grey River's rising waters.

Shantytown, 12km (7.5 miles) south of Greymouth, is a reconstructed 19th-century gold rush town. A train drawn by a steam locomotive takes visitors past gold workings where sluicing is demonstrated and where it is possible to try panning for the elusive metal.

The Mirror Lake

New Zealand's most popular calendar photograph is probably that of the mountains and forest of south Westland reflected flawlessly in the waters of **Lake Matheson**. This is a glacial lake, 6km (3.7 miles) west of Fox Glacier, just off Cook Flat Road. Encircled by native forest, Lake Matheson's mirrored mountains are best photographed in the early morning, before the wind gets up and ruffles its waters.

Hokitika became a boom town and port in the 1860s, despite the natural hazards of its river mouth bar. Gold brought thousands of prospectors. The town's fortunes waned after the gold fever passed and was replaced first by farming and timber milling, then adventure- and eco-tourism. Kayaking and heli-rafting are possible on the swift rivers inland from the town. In the town itself, the **West Coast Historical Museum** has displays of gold-mining methods and equipment, and also many **craft shops**. Hokitika is becoming centre for arts and crafts, with many quality shops and galleries within the town.

Some 30km (19 miles) south of Hokitika is **Ross**, where New Zealand's **largest gold nugget** (almost 2.8kg, or 100oz) was found in 1907. Ross was the site of one of the richest goldfields. There is a historic Goldfields Walkway through the old workings, and a replica of 'The Honourable Roddy', as the nugget was named (after the Minister of Mines), in the Ross Information Centre. You can stop for a whitebait sandwich (in season of course) at the Roddy Nugget Café.

After Ross, SH6 swings inland and shadows the foothills of the Southern Alps to Franz Josef. Along the way is a fork road to **Okarito Lagoon**, New Zealand's largest unmodified tidal inlet and a major feeding ground for birds (over 70 species), including the **white heron** or **kotuku**. The herons breed at a sanctuary near the Whataroa River, at the northern end of the lagoon. You can visit the breeding site with local tourist operators who hold a concession permit to enter into the colony. Okarito's other famous inhabitant is author **Keri Hulme**, who won the Booker Prize in 1985 for her novel ***the bone people***, the setting for which is the local area.

After **Franz Josef** and **Fox glaciers**, SH6 traverses the mountains and rain forests of **Westland National Park**, then veers inland at the **Haast River** mouth. Thereafter it traces the river valley through the **Haast Pass** (an ancient greenstone-seeking route for Maori) to **Lake Wanaka** and Central Otago, in the process passing from one of New Zealand's wettest regions to its driest.

Wild Food Festival

New Zealand has many food festivals, but there is nothing quite like the Wild Food Festival held in **Hokitika** on the second Saturday in March. A celebration of 'bush tucker', many stalls sell feral temptations such as venison, goat, wild pork, possum, eel, the local delicacy, whitebait, and also huhu grubs (the larvae of a forest insect) and farmed worms. This 'bush tucker' is accompanied by locally brewed beer, South Island wines and rousing traditional items by idiosyncratic West Coast bands.

Below: *The awe-inspiring Fox Glacier is one of the top attractions on New Zealand's West Coast.*

The Wild West Coast at a Glance

Best Times To Visit

This region has a high average rainfall year-round, but enjoys a mild, temperate climate. The months of **mid-winter** (June–July), and **summer** (January–February) traditionally have the least rain. Outdoor activities can be enjoyed year-round, but you should always pack wet-weather gear and be prepared to be exposed to the elements during your visit.

Getting There

This formerly remote area can now be reached via scenic accessways. By **road** these are through the Buller Gorge from Nelson, Lewis Pass via Reefton, Arthur's Pass from Christchurch, or the Haast Pass from Queenstown, in the south. The **airports** at **Westport** and **Hokitika** offer regular scheduled services to other centres in the North and the South Island, while the **TranzAlpine Express** connection between Christchurch and Greymouth is considered one of the world's great **train** journeys. **Intercity**, **Coast to Coast Shuttles**, **Alpine Coach and Couriers**, **Atomic Shuttles** and **East West Coaches** all provide links to other regions.

Getting Around

The West Coast is ideal for driving, with well-maintained roads and light traffic. **Car rentals** are available in all major towns (Westport, Greymouth, and Hokitika). A **taxi** service is also available in Westport and Greymouth. Otherwise, InterCity and Mt Cook Landline run daily **coach** services in both directions between Nelson and Queenstown, passing right along the West Coast, with an overnight stop at the glacier villages.

Where to Stay

The West Coast has a range of quality bed and breakfasts, hotels, motels, backpackers, farmstays and holiday parks.

Northern West Coast

Mid-range

The Last Resort, PO Box 31, Karamea, tel: (03) 782 6617, fax: (03) 782 6820, web: www. lastresort.co.nz A small farming community, Karamea offers end-of-the-road relaxation; The Last Resort has a wide range of accommodation and quality dining.

Central West Coast

Budget

Formerly the Blackball Hilton, Hart St, Blackball, tel: (03) 732 4705, fax: (03) 732 4708, e-mail: bbhilton@xtra.co.nz web: www.blackballhilton.co.nz A character bed and breakfast; lively events calendar.

Railway Hotel, 120 Mawhera Quay, Greymouth, tel: (03) 768 7023, fax: (03) 768 7026. Accommodation and meals in the Kiwi railway tradition.

Southland Hotel, 111 Revell St, Hokitika, tel: (03) 755 8344, fax: (03) 755 8258, reservations: 0800 400 344, e-mail: southland@clear.net.nz web: www.southlandhotel.com Twenty-three full facility rooms and a restaurant with panoramic views of the Tasman Sea.

Where to Eat

The Smelting House Café, 102 Mackay St, Greymouth, tel: (03) 768 0012, fax: (03) 768 0075. Home-made breakfasts, lunches and in-betweens, produced with flair.

South Westland Salmon and **The Salmon Farm Café**, Lake Paringa Postal Agency, South Westland, tel/fax: (03) 751 0837, e-mail: salmonfarm@xtra.co.nz A salmon farm where visitors can feed the salmon and buy salmon products. The café specializes in salmon dishes.

Tours and Excursions

Alpine Guides Fox Glacier, PO Box 38, Fox Glacier, tel: (03) 751 0825, fax: (03) 751 0857, e-mail: foxguides@mindata.co.nz web: www.nz-holiday.co.nz/foxguides This mainstream adventure operator offers a range of guided excursions onto the Fox Glacier.

Franz Josef Glacier Guides, PO Box 4, Franz Josef, tel: (03) 752 0763, fax: (03) 752 0102, e-mail: glacierguides@minidata.co.nz A spectacular glacier experience. Travel amid the most magnificent and challenging glacial environment available to the general public in the world.

The Wild West Coast at a Glance

Kea West Coast Tours, 152 Golf Links Rd, Greymouth, tel: (03) 768 9292, freephone: 0800 532 868, fax: (03) 768 0492, e-mail: info@keatours.co.nz web: www.keatours.co.nz Guided tours of the West Coast and introduction to regional fauna and flora.

Norwest Adventures Ltd, 182 Queen St, Westport, tel: (03) 789 6686, freephone: 0800 11 66 86, e-mail: norwest@xtra.co.nz web: www.voyager.co.nz/-schurr/nwa.html Both the original 'Underworld Rafting' and the 'Metro Cave Tour' combine mystery and intrigue amidst stunning formations and the best glow-worm displays in the enormous Metro Cave. Trips twice daily.

Off Beat Tours, Atarau, RD 1, Blackball, Westland, tel: (03) 732 3749, freephone: 0800 270 960, fax: (03) 732 3749, e-mail: kmdash@xtra.co.nz Professionally guided small group eco-nature tours of the West Coast. Discover dynamic glaciers, beautiful lakes, wild coastline scenery, wildlife, rain forest, flora and fauna.

On Yer Bike! Coal Creek, State Highway 6, Greymouth, tel: (03) 762 7438, freephone: 0800 669372, web: www.onyerbike.co.nz Four-wheel bike and eight-wheel argo adventure tours through beautiful native forest and farmland. There are tours for all ages and adventure levels.

White Heron Sanctuary Tours, SH6, Whataroa, tel: (03) 753 4120, fax (03) 753 4087, freephone: 0800 523 456, e-mail info@whiteherontours.co.nz web: www.whiteherontours.co.nz Visit New Zealand's only white heron (kotuku) breeding colony. Accommodation is available.

Fox and Franz Josef Heliservices, Alpine Guides Building, Main Rd, Fox Glacier, tel: (03) 751 0866, and Alpine Adventure Centre, Main Rd, Franz Josef, tel: (03) 752 0793, fax: (03) 752 0764. Helicopter flights over the glaciers, as well as hunting, fishing, kayaking and rafting. Reservations: 0800 800 793, e-mail: Fox_Heli@xtra.co.nz web: www.scenic-flights.co.nz

Useful Contacts

Tourism West Coast, 1st floor, Regent Theatre Building, Mackay St, Greymouth, tel: (03) 768 6633, fax: (03) 768 7680, e-mail: tourismwc@minidata.co.nz web: www.west-coast.co.nz

Karamea Information and Resource Centre, Bridge St, PO Box 94, Karamea, tel: (03) 782 6652, fax: (03) 782 6654.

Westport Information Centre, 1 Brougham St, Westport, tel/fax: (03) 789 6658, e-mail: westport.info@xtra.co.nz web: www.westport.org.nz

Punakaiki Visitor Centre, Paparoa National Park, Department of Conservation, SH6, PO Box 1, Punakaiki, tel: (03) 731 1895, fax: (03) 731 1888, e-mail: punakaikivc@doc.govt.nz

Greymouth Information Centre, cnr Mackay and Herbert streets, PO Box 95, Greymouth, tel: (03) 768 5101, fax: (03) 768 0317, e-mail: vingm@minidata.co.nz web: www.westcoastbookings.co.nz

Westland Visitor Information Centre, cnr Hamilton and Tancred streets, PO Box 171, Hokitika, tel: (03) 755 6166, fax: (03) 755 5011, e-mail: hkkvin@xtra.co.nz

Franz Josef Visitor Centre, Department of Conservation, SH6, PO Box 14, Franz Josef, tel: (03) 752 0796, fax: (03) 752 0797, e-mail: vctemp@doc.govt.nz

Fox Glacier Visitors Centre, Department of Conservation, SH6, Fox Glacier, tel: (03) 751 0807, fax: (03) 751 0858, web: www.glaciercountry.co.nz

HOKITIKA	J	F	M	A	M	J	J	A	S	O	N	D
AVE. TEMP. °C	16	16	15	12	10	8	8	8	10	12	13	15
AVE. TEMP. °F	61	61	59	54	50	46	46	46	50	54	55	59
AVE. RAINFALL mm	262	191	239	236	244	231	218	239	226	292	267	262
AVE. RAINFALL in	10.3	7.5	9.4	9.3	9.6	9.1	8.6	9.4	8.9	11.5	10.5	10.3

Regent

9
Dunedin and the Deep South

Often bypassed by visitors, the southernmost region of the South Island nevertheless has some unique attractions. Dunedin is a city of unexpected delights; the Catlin's State Forest Park is one of New Zealand's loveliest wilderness areas, and Stewart Island, though not often visited, makes a strong impression on those who see it. In the far southwest, Fiordland offers some of the country's most majestic mountain scenery and seascapes.

Dunedin and Around

A historic city with a **Scottish heritage**, Dunedin (population 107,088) has a unique combination of cultural and natural appeal. Capital of the Otago region, it is sited at the head of a long, sheltered harbour, with the **Otago Peninsula** alongside it. Settlement began in 1848, and its Scottish founders gave it the ancient Gaelic name for Edinburgh. The discovery of **gold** in Central Otago in 1861 brought thousands of fortune-hunters to the region, and the wealth generated by the gold and this influx made Dunedin **the commercial capital** of New Zealand for the next two decades.

Today the compact, congenial city climbs from its harbour up to a rim of hills, along the peninsula and across to the open Pacific coast. Now foremostly a **tertiary education centre**, Dunedin's economy is based on thriving **University of Otago** and the vitality and capital brought to the city by its 19,000 students, known locally as 'scarfies'. The city's Victorian heritage is evident in its many **fine stone buildings** and **cultural centres**: museums, an art

Don't Miss

*** **Fiordland National Park:** the largest in the country and a World Heritage area.
*** **Larnach Castle:** set on a hill with commanding views over the Otago Peninsula.
*** **Tairoa Head:** the world's only mainland breeding colony of the northern royal albatross.
** **Olveston:** perhaps New Zealand's finest historic home, in Dunedin.
** **Catlin's State Forest Park:** a wildlife area of mountains and coastline.
** **Stewart Island:** the third largest island in New Zealand.

Opposite: *The Octagon in central Dunedin is near all the town's main attractions.*

gallery, libraries, the university and New Zealand's only castle. Yet only a short drive away, at the end of the Otago Peninsula, some of the country's most precious forms of **wildlife** – yellow-eyed penguins and royal albatrosses – thrive in their natural habitat. This unique blend makes Dunedin a special place which visitors invariably find memorable.

Above: *Larnach Castle is just a short distance from Dunedin city, on the Otago Peninsula.*
Opposite: *Dunedin's splendidly restored Victorian railway station*

Central Dunedin is ideal for exploring **on foot**, as nowhere is more than 15 minutes' walk from the **Octagon**, in the middle of the central business district. Around the Octagon are the refurbished **Dunedin Public Art Gallery, St Paul's Anglican Cathedral**, the **Municipal Chambers**, the **Visitor Information Centre** and a number of **cafés**. The statue of poet **Robbie Burns** overlooking the Octagon testifies to the city's Scottish ancestry, while on either side of his likeness is **Writers' Walk** – plaques inscribed with quotations from the works of many eminent New Zealand writers who have found literary inspiration in Dunedin.

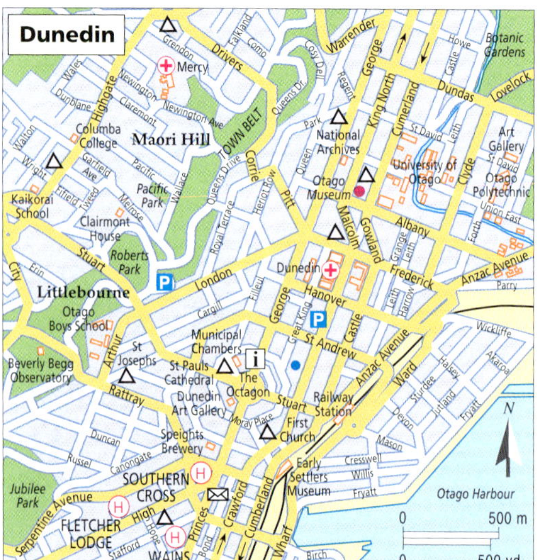

Leading eastwards off the Octagon is **George Street**, the main shopping thoroughfare, and to the southeast is the original buildings of the University of Otago (1869), New Zealand's oldest such institution. The **Hocken Library**, one of the finest research libraries in New Zealand, formerly found within the university, is now located in a separate building on Anzac Avenue. **Dunedin Railway Station** (1906) is another excellent example of Victorian architecture, while the **First Church of Otago** (1873), with its soaring stone spire, is a conspicuous city landmark. The social history of the region is displayed in the **Otago Settlers Museum**, south of the Octagon. In Rattray Street is **Speight's Brewery**, one of the oldest in the country, which can be toured. The **Botanic Garden**, with its rose and rhododendron beds, lies at the northern end of the city, while **Carisbrook**, Dunedin's famous rugby and cricket ground (known to visiting teams as the 'House of Pain' because of the punishment they invariably receive at the hands of the Otago players), is on the southern side.

Few other New Zealand cities have such a range of easily accessible attractions in their immediate vicinity as Dunedin. **St Clair**, **St Kilda** and **Tomahawk Beach** are white sand ocean surf beaches just to the south, **Larnach Castle** is 13km (8 miles) to the east, and historic **Port Chalmers** lies across the harbour, 12km (7.5 miles) from the Octagon. The unique and endangered yellow-eyed penguin colony can be viewed from special hides at **Penguin Place**, a conservation reserve near the end of the Otago Peninsula, 50 minutes' drive from the central city, while **Tairoa Head** and its royal albatross colony are only five minutes further along the road.

Taieri Gorge Railway

An excursion not to be missed is the **day train trip** from Dunedin up the Taieri Gorge to Pukerangi and back. Engineered brilliantly during the Victorian era, the line crosses wrought-iron viaducts and passes through hand-hewn tunnels, becoming more and more spectacular the further up the gorge it climbs, with **breathtaking views** of the gold-bearing Taieri River and schist rock formations. The modern, comfortable train leaves Dunedin Railway Station at 14:30 from October to March, returning at 18:30; or it leaves at 12:30 from April to September, returning at 16:30.

The Southern Scenic Route

The 440km (273-mile) Southern Scenic Route begins in Dunedin. It incorporates some of the most scenic and least populated regions of New Zealand, ideal for visitors to absorb the southern region's unspoiled beauty. The route first crosses the rolling hills of **South Otago**, following the coast to **Taieri Mouth**, before turning inland and passing through the undistinguished town of **Balclutha**, near the mouth of the Clutha River, then through **Catlins State Forest**

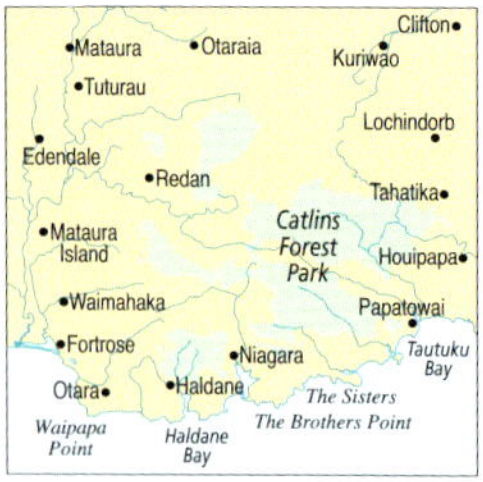

A Cruise on the Wild Side

Monarch takes visitors right into the Otago Peninsula's wildlife environment and ecosystem. The boat leaves daily from the corner of Wharf and Fryatt streets in the city and calls at Wellers Rock on the peninsula before cruising around Tairoa Head, allowing close viewing of wading birds, the royal albatross nesting area, the fur seal colony, penguins, shags (cormorants) and the headland's dramatic geological formations.

Park, which occupies the southeastern extremity of the South Island. Turning to the west at Papatowai, the route crosses the lush **Southland Plains**, passes through **Invercargill** and western Southland before veering north at **Te Waewae Bay** and leading directly on to **Manapouri** and **Te Anau**.

Catlins State Forest Park **

This park is an area where mountains covered with stands of native podocarp forest interface with the Pacific Ocean. The park begins at Nugget Point in South Otago and extends 85km (53 miles) southwest to the sprocket-like Waipapa Point in Southland. The southeasterly ocean winds and wind-driven waves have relentlessly gnawed into this coast, eroding the sedimentary rock into bays and promontories, inlets and beaches, caves and cliffs – a landscape inhospitable to humans but a wonderful environment for **sea birds**, **seals**, **sea lions** and **penguins**. **Dolphins** and migrating **whales** inhabit the coastal waters, while just inland, the stands of rimu, rata and beech forest provide a precious habitat for native birds such as the **tui**, **bellbird**, **fantail** and **red-crowned parakeeti**.

At **Nugget Point**, a rocky promontory, a path leading to a lighthouse affords spectacular ocean views. The point is home to New Zealand fur seals, southern elephant seals, Hooker sea lions, sooty shearwaters, the rare yellow-eyed penguin or *hoiho*, shags and other seabirds. In **Owaka** township, some 12km (7.5 miles) further south, there is a small museum with displays of the Catlins pioneer history, mainly the plundering of the whales, seals and forests. The Catlins Visitor Centre and a Department of Conservation Field Centre in Owaka provide interesting information on the park's natural and human history.

Below: *Yellow-eyed penguins in their natural habitat, Otago Peninsula.*

In the vicinity of the village of **Papatowai** there are forest and beach walks as well as accommodation and, since it is near the midway point on the road through the park, Papatowai makes a very good base for exploring. The Old Coach Track/ Tahakopa Loop Track passes through coastal podocarp forest on the edge of a sandy bay, to what was once a moa hunter camp at the river mouth. At **Tautuku Bay**, a superb sandy beach, a boardwalk takes visitors out onto a pristine estuary, while there are glorious views of the area's forest and coastline from Florence Hill Lookout, above the bay.

Waikawa, towards the southern end of the Catlins, has a sheltered harbour, from which dolphin encounter charters operate. About 10km (6 miles) south of Waikawa is **Curio Bay** and a distinctive geological feature of the Catlins, a Jurassic fossilized forest that is visible at low tide. Fossil forests are rare, and are necessarily protected. The one at Curio Bay can be seen

Above: *The Otago Peninsula provides a superb habitat for animals such as the southern fur seal.*

by following the track to the beach at low tide, and walking across a rocky shelf which is actually the forest floor. The remains of petrified trees embedded in rock prove that 180 million years ago, when most of New Zealand was under sea, this area was a forest-covered lowland. This fossil forest is considered one of the world's finest.

Waipapa Point, at the western end of the Catlins, is the site of New Zealand's worst shipwreck. Here, in 1881, 131 lives were lost when *SS Tararua* foundered. Today the exposed and windswept point is home to sea lions and seals.

Invercargill and Southland

The most southerly city in New Zealand, **Invercargill** (population 57,000) was founded by Scots in the 1850s and built in a grid pattern on a large area beside a wide estuary. They named the streets after rivers in the **Scottish Highlands**. Later, the town also became home to immigrants from Ireland. Some of the 19th-century Oamaru stone buildings remain. Like Otago people, Southlanders still retain a distinctive Scots burr in the 'r' sounds of their speech.

The founders of Invercargill endowed it with several parks and reserves. Most prominent is **Queens Park**, a botanical reserve that includes a rose garden, wildlife

Above: *The war memorial in Invercargill.*
Opposite: *A waterfall in Fiordland National Park.*

The Bluff Oyster

Foveaux Strait's great gift to the gourmet world is the Bluff Oyster. This **deepwater shellfish** is dredged from the bottom of the strait from the beginning of March to the end of August, processed locally, then flown to shops and restaurants all over New Zealand. Connoisseurs rate the sweet, succulent Bluff Oyster as the world's finest, particularly when eaten straight from the shell. Bluff holds an **Oyster Festival** in **May**, about a month after the oyster season begins.

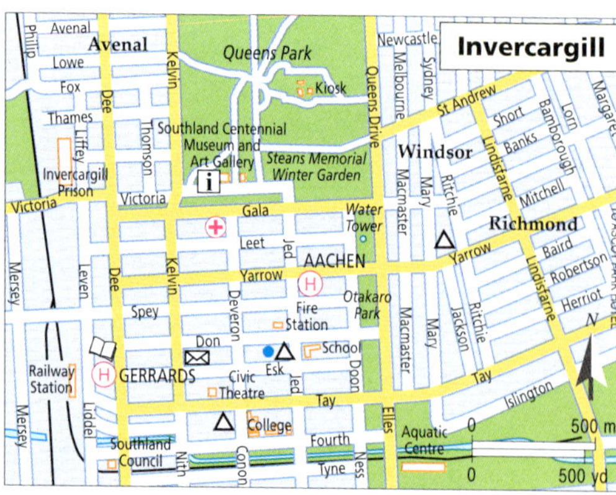

sanctuary and Steans Memorial Winter Garden. Near the park's entrance is the Southland Museum, Art Gallery and Observatory. **Oreti Beach**, just west of the city, is a long stretch of sand, backed by lupin-covered dunes, a popular spot in summer for swimming and other water sports.

Some 25km (15 miles) southeast of Invercargill, at the tip of a peninsula, is the port of **Bluff**, which handles a large export trade. It is also the base for the **fishing fleet** which dredges Foveaux Strait for the famous Bluff oysters, and a shipping service which takes passengers and supplies across the strait to Halfmoon Bay on Stewart Island. Across a narrow stretch of water from Bluff is **Tiwai Point**, New Zealand's only aluminium smelter, which processes aluminium oxide from Queensland, using hydro-electric power generated by the Lake Manapouri power station.

The Southland town of **Gore**, 58km (36 miles) northeast of Invercargill, straddles the Mataura River and is overlooked by the Hokonui Hills. The district is renowned for its **trout fishing** and Gore prides itself on being the brown trout capital of the world. There is a statue of a trout in the centre of town. Gore's other claim to fame is that it is the nation's **country music capital**, a status celebrated in late May and early June by the Gold Guitar Awards, when country music aficionados demonstrate their talents.

The Tuatapere Hump Ridge Track is a 53km (33 miles), three-day tramp which begins and ends at Rarakau Farm, on Te Waewae Bay, in west Southland. The track climbs through beech forest, often on boardwalks, to 900m (2953 feet), giving superb views of surrounding rock formations and mountains. Described as 'real *Lord of the Rings* territory', the track can be visited on the website: www.humpridgetrack.co.nz or contact Kiwi Wilderness walks, tel: 0800 733 549.

THE KINGSTON FLYER

Those visitors who remember with deep affection the era of the **steam train** can exercise their nostalgia with a trip on the *Kingston Flyer*, a restored coal-fired 'Ab' class locomotive which runs between the Southland town of **Fairlight**, on SH6, and **Kingston**, at the southern tip of Lake Wakatipu. The vintage train with its Victorian carriages, including a refreshment car, plies the route three times daily from 1 October to 30 April. The return trip takes just under two hours. Web: www.kingstonflyer.co.nz

FIORDLAND

New Zealand's most remote and dramatic region lies in its far southwest, the area ancient Maori knew as **Te Wahipounamu** (the place of greenstone), known today as Fiordland.

THE MILFORD TRACK

Often termed 'the finest walk in the world', the 54km (33.5-mile) four-day Milford Track extends from the head of **Lake Te Anau** to **Milford Sound**, following glaciated valleys, ascending an alpine pass, and traversing some stunningly lovely glaciated terrain before following the shore of **Lake Ada** to reach **Sandfly Point**. Although the track has become excessively popular for those wishing to make a total escape from the madding crowd, it is still one of the best equipped, maintained and directed of New Zealand's wilderness walks. The season extends from November through to April.

Fiordland National Park is the largest in the country, covering 12,500km^2 (7750 sq miles). In 1990, about 2.6 million ha (6.4 million acres) of the southwest of the South Island was declared a **World Heritage Area**, giving international recognition to its outstanding natural value.

Shaped by glaciers of the last **Ice Age**, Fiordland has immense **geographic grandeur** – sheer-sided fiords, U-shaped valleys, hanging valleys, icy lakes, beech forests and towering mountains. This is home to one of the world's rarest birds, the flightless takahe. It is **New Zealand's wettest region**, receiving over 12,800mm (4922in) of rain a year in some areas, while Sutherland Falls, at 580m (1902ft), is the country's highest waterfall.

Milford Sound **

Most accessible of Fiordland's natural attractions is Milford Sound, reached by road or air from Queenstown or Te Anau. The drive from Te Anau to Milford along SH94 and through the Homer Tunnel is one of New Zealand's most **scenic routes**.

Scenic flights can be taken over the area surrounding Milford Sound, which is also a popular calling place for cruise ships (the waters of the sound are so deep that ships cannot anchor in it, and must keep their engines running). A **cruise** on the sound is the best way to fully appreciate its grandeur. Newest of the vessels cruising the sound is the purpose-built 40m (131ft) *Milford Mariner*, which has overnight accommodation in cabins. Milford Sound is like an enclosed world, misty and brooding, and bordered by towering walls of rock down which cataracts tumble and to which rainforest clings. At 1694m (5556ft), **Mitre Peak**

Below: *MacKinnon's Pass is the highest point on the scenic Milford Track.*

(named after a bishop's head-dress) dominates the skyline above Milford Sound. In the depths of the sound's shaded waters, black corals thrive.

Te Anau **

Te Anau lies on the shores of **Lake Te Anau**, New Zealand's second largest lake. The town is located close to Fiordland's main walking tracks – the Milford, Hollyford, Routeburn and Greenstone Tracks – while the Kepler Track begins and ends at Te Anau. A unique geological attraction of the area is the **Te Anau Caves**, a 30-minute boat trip across the lake to the cave system on its western shore. The natural incandescence of thousands of glow-worms on the cave walls is a magical sight.

For the engineering-minded, a trip by boat across **Lake Manapouri**, which is situated to the southwest of Te Anau, to West Arm, and then by coach down a spiral tunnel hewn from solid rock, to the machine hall of the **Manapouri Power Station**, is a stirring excursion. A scheme that proposed to raise the level of Lake Manapouri in the late 1960s and early 1970s to generate more electricity was successfully opposed by the public.

Doubtful Sound and **Deep Cove** are reached by boat across Lake Manapouri then road via the **Wilmot Pass**. Doubtful Sound (so named by Captain James Cook in 1770 because he doubted his ability to sail out again safely if he entered it) is home to frolicking **bottlenose dolphins**, **fur seals** and rare **Fiordland crested penguins**. You can take a cruise or kayaking expedition on Doubtful Sound to observe these creatures.

The most remote and longest of the fiords is **Dusky Sound**, which provided an anchorage and haven for James Cook's *Resolution* during his second southern voyage in 1773. Dusky Sound can be reached via the remote and testing **Dusky Track**, and an ecologically sensitive cruise or kayaking trip then taken on its waters.

Above: *A comfortable cruise ship on the deep waters of Milford Sound.*

THE HOLLYFORD TRACK

Following the 80km (50-mile) long valley of the Hollyford, this 54km (33.5-mile) four-day track follows mostly level land from the point where the **Hollyford Valley** road ends, through to the windswept sand dunes of **Martin's Bay**. The track is mainly one-way, but is surrounded by alpine scenery and virgin native forest.

Above: *The view from Stewart Island towards neighbouring Iona Island.* **Opposite:** *The rare harlequin gecko can be found on Stewart Island.*

STEWART ISLAND

Few New Zealanders have visited the country's third largest island, though pre-European Maori knew it as a valuable source of food. They called the island **Rakiura**, which means 'land of glowing skies', probably a reference to displays of the Aurora Australis seen in the night sky over the island. At between 46° and 47° south latitude, Stewart Island is closer to Antarctica than any other permanently inhabited New Zealand territory.

Buffeted by the westerly winds of the 'Roaring Forties', its **climate** is **oceanic**: wet but relatively mild. The west of the island receives up to 5000mm (195in) of rain annually, and Halfmoon Bay, on the eastern side, 1600mm (62in). Composed mainly of granite, Stewart Island is 1740km^2 (1079 sq miles) in size, including its several satellite islands. The island's long coastline is deeply indented, its interior rugged and forested. The highest point is **Mount Anglem**, at 980m (3214ft)

Its relative isolation means that Stewart Island is closer to its **natural state** than any other inhabited New Zealand island. The population of about 500 is clustered about Halfmoon Bay at **Oban**, the only settlement, and beyond Halfmoon Bay and Horseshoe Bay, 2km (1.2 miles) to the north, there are few roads. There are tramping tracks aplenty, however, to take the hiker deep into the island's interior and across to its lonely west coast.

Nearly all of the island consists of **nature reserves** or **scenic reserves**, administered by the Department of Conservation. Its environments include coastal marshes, sand dunes, scrubland, grassland, forests and alpine herbfields. The **forests** are composed mainly of the podocarps kahikatea (white pine) and rimu (red pine), totara and miro, and the flowering trees the kamahai and southern rata. The island's flora is extremely diverse. There are an estimated 160 different plant communities and 28 endemic plant species, most of the latter herbs or dwarf shrubs in the upland zone.

THE RAKIURA TRACK

Of the 250km (155 miles) of walking tracks on Stewart Island, the best is the Rakiura, a 36km (22-mile) three-day track which can be walked in either direction and which immerses the walker in the **unique flora and fauna** of the island. Starting and ending at **Oban**, the track follows the coast, climbs a 300m (984ft) forested ridge and crosses the shores of **Paterson's Inlet**, which deeply indents the island's eastern coast. Boardwalks cover the boggy sections of the track, making the going easier as well as protecting the forest floor. The Rakiura Great Walk is considered one of New Zealand's finest.

Muttonbirding

For centuries **Maori** visited Stewart Island to harvest its paua, crayfish and blue cod. They also seasonally gathered the chicks of the sooty shearwater, or *titi*, as Maori called them. Cooked and preserved in their own fat, the birds were a valuable **winter food source**, as it was too cold to grow the *kumara* (sweet potato). Their common name is muttonbird. In October they migrate in their millions to southern islands of New Zealand to breed. Today the muttonbird season runs from 1 April to 31 May, when Rakiura Maori have the right to visit the islands and take thousands of the young birds.

In spite of the predations of introduced rats and cats, the island's native fauna has survived, albeit precariously. The beautiful and highly endangered **kakapo**, a flightless parrot, has been transferred to outlying Codfish Island for its own protection. The **brown kiwi** of Stewart Island is a recognized subspecies and, uniquely in New Zealand, can sometimes be seen feeding during daylight hours. The island's forests are home to the **kaka** and **kakariki**, members of the parrot family, while the endangered New Zealand **dotterel** breeds not by the sea shore, as it does in other parts of the country, but in the alpine zone. Around the long coastline **penguins**, **petrels**, **shags** and **sooty shearwaters** abound, and whales, seals and dolphins also frequent the island's waters.

Stewart Island can be reached by **ferry** from Bluff twice daily, a one-hour trip, or by **light plane** from Invercargill Airport three times a day, a 20-minute flight.

Dunedin and the Deep South at a Glance

Best Times To Visit

This is New Zealand's coldest lowland region. Rain falls all year, and **summer** temperatures are 25–28°C (77–82°F). Heavy frosts occur in **winter**, and snow falls on the Dunedin hills and parts of Otago and Southland, but at the coast and Stewart Island the sea moderates temperatures.

Getting There

Dunedin Airport is 22km (13.5 miles) south of the city, just off SH1. There are regular flights from Dunedin to Christchurch, Wellington, Rotorua and Auckland, also to Brisbane and Sydney. Four **rental car** agencies are at the airport.
In Anzac Square is **Dunedin Railway Station**.
State Highway 1 goes through Dunedin and Invercargill.

Getting Around

The best way around Dunedin is **on foot**. Get a 'walk sheet' from Dunedin Visitor Centre. **Citibus Newton Ltd** offer bus services around Dunedin and the Otago Peninsula; routes meet at the Octagon. They also run tours of the city and its districts. **Newton Tours** links the scenic attractions of the South Island with Dunedin: **Citisights** buses depart daily from Dunedin Visitor Centre, the Octagon, at 10:00 and 15:30. Newton Tours (Citibus), PO Box 549, Dunedin, tel: (03) 477 5577, fax: (03) 477 8147, e-mail: info@citibus-newton.co.nz

Where to Stay

Dunedin has quality accommodation, from restored heritage hotels to modern lodges, self-catering motels and historic houses, most within a short walk of the Octagon. Most hotels and motels are modern, with full facilities. There are many farmstays in the rural areas of Otago and Southland.

Dunedin

Luxury

Southern Cross Hotel, 118 High St, tel: (03) 477 0752, fax: (03) 477 5776, reservations: 0800 501 616, e-mail: reservations@ southerncrosshotel.co.nz web: www.sceniccircle.co.nz Refurbished Victorian building, with gym, restaurants, bars.
Fletcher Lodge, 276 High St, tel: (03) 477 5552, fax: (03) 474 5551, reservations: 0800 843 563, e-mail: admin@ fletcherlodge.co.nz Former family home of Dunedin industrialist Sir James Fletcher; displays elegance and fine taste throughout.
Lisburn House, 15 Lisburn Ave, Cavershan, tel: (03) 455 8888, fax: (03) 455 6788, e-mail: stay@lisburnhouse.co.nz Restored 19th-century home in garden setting; open fires and four-poster beds.

Te Anau

Mid-range

Luxmore Hotel, in centre of Te Anau township, tel: (03) 249 7526, fax: (03) 249 7272, reservations: 0800 589 667. A range of accommodation, with conference facilities.

Invercargill

Mid-range

Ascot Park Hotel, cnr Tay St and Racecourse Rd, Invercargill, tel: (03) 217 6195, fax: (03) 217 7002, reservations: 0800 272 687, e-mail: ascot@ilt.co.nz web: www.ilt.co.nz Hotel-motel complex; indoor pool.

Stewart Island

Mid-range

Stewart Island Lodge, PO Box 5, Halfmoon Bay, Stewart Island, tel/fax: (03) 219 1085, e-mail: Doug&Margaret@xtra.co.nz web: www.StewartIslandLodge.co.nz
In bush setting, with centrally heated rooms, gourmet meals.

Where to Eat

Dunedin city has over 140 restaurants, cafés and bistros. New Zealand cuisine is prominent, but there are also ethnic restaurants. Pub lunches are excellent.

Dunedin

Luxury

Restaurant Ninety Five, 95 Filleul St, Dunedin, tel: (03) 471 9265. Intimate dining in a character house with courtyard; Central Otago wines.

Mid-range

Etrusco at the Savoy, 8a Moray Place, Dunedin, tel: (03) 477 3737, web: www.ilt.co.nz Quality pizzeria in the historic Savoy Hotel.

Dunedin and the Deep South at a Glance

1908 Café and Bar, 7 Harrington Point Rd, Portobello, tel: (03) 478 0801. Dine in a historic house on the Otago Peninsula, beside the harbour.

Tours and Excursions

Citisights Tour of the Otago Peninsula and Larnach Castle, along Otago Harbour, then to the historic mansion of William Larnach. Tours depart Dunedin Visitor Centre, The Octagon, noon daily; tel: (03) 477 5577, fax: (03) 477 8147.

Olveston Historic Home, 42 Royal Terrace, Dunedin, tel: (03) 477 3320, fax: (03) 479 2094. One-hour guided tours of this magnificent home's antiquities, six times a day, from 09:30.

Back to Nature Wildlife Tour, tel: (03) 474 3300, e-mail: bookings@backtonaturetours.co.nz web: www.backtonaturetours.co.nz Small group (maximum nine) tours of Otago Peninsula's wildlife: albatross, yellow-eyed penguins and sea lions.

Monarch Wildlife Cruises, cnr Wharf and Fryatt streets, Dunedin, tel: (03) 477 4276, fax: (03) 477 4216, e-mail: monarch@wildlife.co.nz web: nz.com/travel/monarch Daily cruises of Otago Peninsula on small ship; view native fauna.

Taieri Gorge Railway, tel: (03) 477 4449, fax: (03) 477 4953, e-mail: reserve@taieri.co.nz web: www.taieri.co.nz Rail journey from Dunedin to the interior of Otago, in a train with all modern comforts. Can be combined with a coach trip to Queenstown.

Catlins Coastal Link, tel: (03) 214 6243, fax: (03) 218 4415, e-mail info@CatlinsCoaster.co.nz web: www.CatlinsCoaster.co.nz Daily guided tours of Catlins area: Catlins Coast, Nugget Point and Curio Bay.

Catlins Natural Wonders, RD2, Owaka, tel/fax: (03) 415 8613, e-mail: catlinw@es.co.nz web: www.es.co.nz/-catlinw/home.htm Eco-tours of the Catlins, with homestay at Papatowai.

Fiordland Travel, PO Box 94, Queenstown and PO Box 1, Te Anau (Head Office), tel: (03) 249 7816, fax: (03) 249 7817, e-mail: info@fiordlandtravel.co.nz web: www.fiordlandtravel.co.nz Scenic tours on Milford and Doubtful Sounds.

Useful Contacts

Stewart Island Travel (1995) Ltd, tel: (03) 219 1269, fax: (03) 219 1355, e-mail: sam@southnet.co.nz Agents for scenic and fishing trips, and kiwi spotting tours.

Dunedin Visitor Information Centre, Municipal Chambers, 48 The Octagon, PO Box 5457, Dunedin, tel: (03) 474 3300, fax: (03) 474 3311, e-mail: visitor.centre@dcc.govt.nz web:www.cityofdunedin.com

Tourism Dunedin, PO Box 1446, Dunedin; tel: (03) 471 8042, fax: (03) 471 8021, e-mail tourism.dunedin@dcc.govt.nz, web: www.dunedinNZ.com

Central Otago Visitor Information Centre, 22 Centennial Ave, PO Box 56, Alexandra, tel: (03) 448 9515, fax: (03) 440 2061, e-mail: info@tco.org.nz

Fiordland Visitor Centre, Lakefront Drive, Te Anau, tel: (03) 249 8900, e-mail vin@realjourneys.co.nz web: www.fiordland.org.nz

Tourism Southland, PO Box 903, Invercargill, tel: (03) 214 9733, fax: (03) 218 9460, e-mail: tourism@southnet.co.nz web: www.southland.org.nz

Stewart Island Visitor Information Network, Department of Conservation, Main Rd, Halfmoon Bay, tel: (03) 219 0009, fax: (03) 219 003, e-mail stewartislandfc@doc.govt.nz

Invercargill Visitor Information Centre, Private Bag 90104, 108 Gala Street, Invercargill, tel: (03) 214 6243, fax: (03) 218 4415.

DUNEDIN	J	F	M	A	M	J	J	A	S	O	N	D
AVE. TEMP. °C	15	15	14	12	9	7	6	7	9	11	12	14
AVE. TEMP. °F	59	59	57	54	48	44	43	44	48	52	54	57
AVE. RAINFALL mm	86	71	76	71	81	81	79	76	69	76	81	89
AVE. RAINFALL in	3.3	2.7	2.9	2.7	3.1	3.1	3.0	2.9	2.6	2.9	3.1	3.4

Travel Tips

Tourist Information

There are Visitor Information Network centres in over 100 locations throughout New Zealand, indicated by the green *i* logo. They provide up-to-date and objective information about national and local tourist attractions. The **New Zealand Visitor Information Network (VIN)** consists of three categories: **National Visitor Information Centres**. These provide a comprehensive, seven days a week information and booking service including domestic airline ticketing services. **Regional Visitor Information Centres**. These provide a general information and booking service, seven days a week. **Local Visitor Information Centres**. Centres providing local information at least five days per week.

Other services offered by the VIN centres may include itinerary planning and advice, gifts, souvenirs, stamps and phone cards, restaurant information, local events and entertainment, brochures maps and guide books. The VIN website is: www.nztb.govt.nz/visitor/visitor

The main centre addresses of the Visitor Centres are:
Auckland Travel and Information Centre, Atrium-Sky City, cnr Victoria and Federal streets, Auckland, tel: (09) 979 2333, fax: (09) 979 7010, e-mail: reservations@aucklandnz.com
Wellington Visitor Information Centre, 101 Wakefield Street (Civic Square), tel: (04) 802 4860, fax: (04) 802 4863, e-mail: wgtnvisitors@hotmail.com
Christchurch & Canterbury Visitor Centre, Old Chief Post Office, Cathedral Square West, tel: (03) 379 9629, fax: (03) 377 2424, e-mail: info@christchurchnz.net web: www.christchurchnz.net
Dunedin Visitor Centre, 48 The Octagon, tel: (03) 474 3300, fax: (03) 474 3311, e-mail: visitor.centre@dcc.govt.nz
The **Department of Conservation (DOC)** which administers New Zealand's national parks and elementary camp grounds in wilderness areas, also has detailed visitor information at its offices in the parks and in the cities.

Entry Requirements

Visitors to New Zealand must have a passport, valid for three months beyond the intended time of stay. However if the visitor's home country has an embassy or consulate in New Zealand which can renew the passport, one month beyond the time of stay is sufficient. Visitors from the UK are automatically issued with a permit to stay for up to six months, and a three-month permit is granted to citizens of most European countries, Southeast Asian countries, Japan, the USA and Canada. Australian citizens and permanent residents can stay indefinitely. Citizens of other countries must obtain a visa, valid for three months, from a New Zealand embassy. Granting of a visitor permit or tourist visa is dependent on the applicant having evidence of sufficient funds to support him- or herself without working (about NZ$1000 per month), in the form of cash, travellers' cheques, bank draft, statement from a New Zealand bank account, a major credit card, or a friend or relative who is prepared to guarantee the visitor's accommodation and maintenance. The visitor must also have a confirmed onward ticket and right of entry, including necessary visas, to his or her proposed destination. For information on **embassies** based in New Zealand and abroad, contact the Ministry of Foreign Affairs and Trade, e-mail: enquiries@mft.govt.nz

Customs
Some items may not be brought into New Zealand. These include fresh fruit, vegetables, honey and meat, which may contain organisms that could prove a threat to New Zealand's agricultural industries. Goods made from endangered species, such as elephant tusk ivory, whale bone or teeth or coral rocks, cannot be brought into New Zealand, under international agreement. Amnesty bins for prohibited foodstuffs are provided at all ports of entry. Adults over 17 must fill in a Customs Declaration Form on arrival and keep it with them until they leave the Customs Hall. Smuggling, using false receipts, and importing prohibited goods (drugs, weapons, indecent goods) carry the risk of heavy fines, loss of goods or even imprisonment. Arriving passengers are allowed two 1.125 litre bottles of spirits, 4.5 litres wine, and 200 cigarettes duty free. Provided the NZ$700 duty-free goods allowance is not exceeded, two extra bottles of spirits can be imported.

Health Requirements
No vaccinations are required prior to visiting New Zealand.

Domestic Air Travel
The two domestic airlines are **Air New Zealand** and **Qantas New Zealand**, with smaller ones such as Origin Pacific serving regional centres. Internal air fares can be costly, but special fares ('airpasses') are available on most sectors, usually involving advance booking and payment, with other conditions. These special fares can be booked, ticketed and paid for only in New Zealand. All flights within New Zealand are non-smoking. Air New Zealand's web: http://www.airnz.co.nz Bookings: 0800 737 000.

What to Pack
Sunscreen and sun hats are essential, along with insect repellant and hiking boots if tramping is planned.

Money Matters
The **currency** is the New Zealand dollar which is divided into 100 cents. There are NZ$100, NZ$50, NZ$20, NZ$10 and NZ$5 notes, and coins in denominations of NZ$2 and NZ$1 (both gold) and 50, 20 and 5 cents (all silver). The New Zealand dollar has appreciated against major overseas currencies in recent years, but is still below the value of the American and Australian dollars, making shopping in New Zealand good value for visitors from abroad.
A **Goods and Services Tax** (GST) of 12.5% is added to the cost of purchases and services, except those in duty-free shops.
A **departure tax** of NZ$25 is payable when leaving New Zealand for an overseas destination.
The best **exchange rates** are given by the trading banks: BNZ, National Bank, ANZ, Westpac and Postbank. Banks are closed at weekends, but most have 24-hour **ATMs** which require a valid cash card and PIN number. If staying for any duration, it is worth opening a cashcard account with one of the major banks.
A practical boon for shoppers is the **EFTPOS** (Electronic Funds Transfer at Point of Sale) card system. Issued by the trading banks, an EFTPOS card deducts the relevant sum automatically from a local cheque or savings account, after a PIN number is entered. Many EFTPOS holders will also issue cash on request. Most shops (including dairies), petrol stations and restaurants have EFTPOS, enabling you to avoid carrying large amounts of cash, and making the country an almost 'cashless society'.
Tipping is not common, but a tip of 10% can be added to a restaurant bill if the service is considered particularly helpful.

PUBLIC HOLIDAYS

1 January • New Year's Day
2 January • Day after New Year's Day
6 February • Waitangi Day
Good Friday
Easter Sunday
25 April • Anzac Day
First Monday in June • Queen's Birthday
Last Monday in October • Labour Day.
25 December • Christmas Day.
26 December • Boxing Day

Accommodation

The huge growth in tourism in New Zealand has assured every type of accommodation, from de luxe hotels in the cities to Department of Conservation huts in the national parks. Prices are commensurate with the level of comfort. **Luxury hotels** cost from NZ$200–300 per room per night; hostels with shared facilities less than NZ$20 per night, per person. Hostels have proliferated in recent years, and are found everywhere in rural districts as well as in the main cities.
Two prominent chains of **hostel accommodation** are: **VIP Backpacker Resorts International New Zealand**, PO Box 80021, Green Bay, Auckland, tel: (09) 827 6016, fax: (09) 827 6013, e-mail: backpack@vip.co.nz web: www.vip.co.nz and **Budget Backpacker Hostels**, 99 Titiraupenga Street, Taupo, tel/fax: (07) 377 1568, e-mail: bbhcard@backpack.co.nz web: www.backpack.co.nz
YHA New Zealand, part of the international YHA chain, maintains 57 hostels throughout the country. There is 'No Age Limit', 'No Curfews', 'No Duties'. For reservations and information, contact: YHA New Zealand National Reservations Centre, PO Box 436, Christchurch, tel: (03) 379 9808, fax: (03) 379 4415, e-mail: book@yha.org.nz web: www.yha.org.nz
Popular with holiday-making New Zealanders are **motels**. Almost every town has at least one, which has units with sleeping space for two or three people, a bathroom and full kitchen facilities, making the accommodation self-catering. Motels are priced from NZ$70–100 per unit per night for a couple, each additional adult costing an extra NZ$10–14.
Guesthouses and **bed and breakfast** places vary from humble to luxurious. Ordinary guesthouses with shared bathroom facilities average NZ$70 per room per night, and luxury bed and breakfasts (en suite) cost NZ$200–300 per night. Many of these are in beautifully refurbished historic homesteads.
A novel way to enjoy rural life is to stay on a **working farm**, where you can relax and enjoy the scenery, or participate in farm activities. There are also rural homestays or self-catering farm cottages that cost NZ$60–90 for a room per night, including breakfast. Some include dinners on request, at an additional charge of NZ$20–25 per person. For details contact New Zealand Farm Holidays Ltd, PO Box 558, Orewa, Auckland, tel: (09) 426 5430, fax: (09) 426 8474, e-mail: farm@nzaccom.co.nz web: www.nzaccom.co.nz

Good Reading

Duff, Alan (1990) *Once Were Warriors* (Tandem Press).
Frame, Janet (2000) *An Angel at My Table* (Vintage).
King, Michael (2003) *The Penguin History of New Zealand* (Penguin).
Pattrick, Jenny (2003) *The Denniston Rose* (Vintage).

Eating Out

Vegetarians are well catered for in most places. The minimum legal drinking age was lowered to 18 years in 1999. Proof of identity and age must be produced on demand in licensed hotels and bars, otherwise service will be declined.

Driving

Outside the main centres, the roads are uncongested, except during peak holiday periods. Generally the roads are of a good standard except in sparsely populated country districts, with the four centres having motorway systems.
For **State Highway Reports**, call 0900 33 222 (at a charge of NZ$1 per minute).
Drivers are often impatient on the road, so be prepared to drive defensively! Drive on the **left side** of the road. When turning at an intersection, give way to traffic not turning. Give way to all traffic crossing or approaching from your right. When turning left at an intersection and a vehicle coming from the opposite direction is indicating its intention to turn right, you must give way (this is the opposite to the turning rule in many other countries). Speed limits are shown in km/h. Traffic signals are universal: red, amber and green, and there is no amber phase between red and green. Amber also means stop, unless you are so close to the lights that you cannot stop safely. You cannot turn left if the stop light at an intersection is red, unless there is a green arrow pointing left. If there is a free turn left sign at an inter-

section, you must give way to traffic proceeding straight ahead from the right. All occupants of a vehicle, including rear seat passengers and children, must wear **seat belts** at all times, or you will be fined. Motorcyclists and cyclists must wear a **helmet** at all times. No pedestrians or cyclists are allowed on motorways, and stopping of vehicles on motorways is prohibited except in emergencies. The maximum **speed limit** on the open road is 100km/h (60mph), in urban areas 50km/h (30mph). In a Limited Speed Zone (indicated by a circular sign showing the letters LSZ) safe speeds can be affected by weather, road or other conditions. In such zones the speed limit is 50km/h (30mph) in adverse conditions, 100km/h (60mph) in normal conditions. Speed cameras operate in urban and rural areas. If caught exceeding the speed limit on camera you are fined automatically. Yellow lines indicate no overtaking is allowed. There is no parking beside a yellow line or within 6m (10ft) of an intersection. Road hazard signs carry internationally recognized symbols, and are clearly positioned. Temporary hazard signs indicate dangers such as slips, road works or a slippery surface. One-lane bridges are common on rural roads. Approach them cautiously and be prepared to give way. There might be a circular sign showing a small red arrow pointing away from you and a large black arrow pointing towards you. This means that vehicles coming towards you from the other side of the bridge have the right of way. A rectangular blue sign with a large white arrow pointing away from you means you have right of way on the bridge. After crossing the bridge ensure that you move back to the **left side** of the road. Some rural roads are unsealed (or 'metalled'). On such roads corrugations and the build-up of shingle on the edges demand extra care when driving. In winter (June–October) in alpine areas, always carry snow chains. Frosts and snowfalls are common in the inland of both islands. May–October in the South Island and June–September in the North Island is when caution should be exercised in hilly areas. 'Black ice' makes driving hazardous on the Desert Road in the central North Island, especially on the shady sections of the road. Add antifreeze to radiators during winter in regions south of the Bombay Hills. **Don't drink and drive**. The legal limit is 30mg alcohol per 100ml blood for drivers under 20 years, 80mg alcohol per 100ml blood for fully licensed drivers 20 years and over. There is no insurance cover for drivers above the legal limit. Random, compulsory breath testing is done. Penalties for exceeding the blood-alcohol limit are severe, involving heavy fines and loss of licence. If you crash, contact the police. Obtain driver's name, address and registration numbers of all vehicles involved. If you injure an animal, notify the owner, the police or the SPCA at once. Most visitors travel by **rental** car, rental van ('camper-van') or by coach. Agencies like Avis, Budget and Hertz are in all the main airports. A list of agencies is included in the Yellow Pages. Most companies require an International Driver's Licence, and the driver must be over 21. The Automobile Association's website is: www.nzaa.co.nz Addresses and numbers for the AA in the main centres are: **Auckland Central**, 99 Albert Street, tel: (09) 377 4660. **Wellington**, 342-352 Lambton Quay, tel: (04) 470 9999. **Christchurch**, 210 Herford Street, tel: (03) 379 1280. **Dunedin**, 450 Moray Place, tel: (03) 477 5945.

Conversion Chart

From	To	Multiply By
Millimetres	Inches	0.0394
Metres	Yards	1.0936
Metres	Feet	3.281
Kilometres	Miles	0.6214
Square kilometres	Square miles	0.386
Hectares	Acres	2.471
Litres	Pints	1.760
Kilograms	Pounds	2.205
Tonnes	Tons	0.984

To convert Celsius to Fahrenheit: x 9 ÷ 5 + 32

InterCity Coachlines has daily **coaches** on many routes. Auckland, tel: 913 6100; Wellington, tel: 472 5111; Christchurch, tel: 379 9020; Dunedin, tel: 474 9600; web: www.intercitycoach.co.nz
Rent a **camper-van** to tour rural areas. Camper-van companies are near main airports. Two major ones are **Maui** (www.discover.co.nz/maui_nz) and **Brits** (www.brits.co.nz).

Business Hours
Banks are open 09:00–16:30, Mon–Fri. Shopping hours are commonly 09:00–17:30 Mon–Thu, 09:00–20:00 Fri, 09:00–16:00 Sat, 10:00–16:00 Sun. Corner stores ('dairies') are usually open daily 08:00–20:00.

Time Difference
New Zealand is 12 hours ahead of GMT, and uses daylight savings time – clocks go back one hour in late March, and are put forward one hour in early October.

Communications
Public telephone booths take credit cards or phone cards, available from corner stores ('dairies'). Local calls from private telephones are free.
Useful numbers are:
National Directory: **018**
International Directory: **0172**

Electricity
New Zealand operates on 230V AC, 50 hertz mains supply, 3-pin plug and socket system. Most hotels provide 110V AC sockets (20V) for shavers only, and hardware or electronic goods stores stock adaptors.

Weights and Measures
New Zealand uses the metric system.

Health Services
Telephone directories list all emergency services, including **doctors** and **hospitals**, in the front section of the book.

Personal Safety
New Zealand is generally safe, but don't take safety for granted. Violent crime (assault and robbery) has become a problem, mainly in city centres late at night. Tourists are a prime target for criminals. ***Do not walk alone late at night in inner city precincts.*** Tourist vehicles parked at scenic areas can attract thieves' attention. ***Do not leave valuables in vehicles at any time.***
Prepare carefully for tramping at altitude. The weather can change suddenly, with clear skies changing to cloud, cold and rain in minutes. Temperatures drop dramatically at night, even after fine days. Wear strong boots when tramping and pack wet-weather gear, no matter how fine the day is. Leave an itinerary with friends or the police and check the forecast before setting out. For Automatic Weather Forecasts call 0900 99 909.

Health Precautions
There are no poisonous reptiles in New Zealand. Bites come mainly from mosquitoes (common in the north in summer) and sand-flies (at the coast in summer). Buy repellants – roll-on, sprays, burning coils, or a plug-in-the-wall repellant – from pharmacies or hardware stores. The sole poisonous land creature in New Zealand is the katipo spider. The poison from its bite can severely affect the nervous system, but bites are rare. The only poisonous jellyfish is the Portuguese man-of-war, *Physalia physalis*. Many rural streams and rivers are infected with giardia and E-coli, micro-organisms which can cause serious intestinal illness, including diarrhoea and cramps. Thus water from rural streams and rivers should not be drunk untreated.

Emergencies
In an emergency, the number to ring is **111**. The operator will ask which emergency service is required – Ambulance, Fire Service or Police – and the location of the caller.

Etiquette
In summer (February–April), fire bans can be imposed to protect forest areas. Respect bans by not lighting fires, carefully extinguishing cigarettes and not leaving behind any broken glass, which can ignite fire in very hot conditions.

Language
Both English and Maori are the official languages.

USEFUL MAORI PHRASES

Kia ora • Hello or good health
Tena Koe • Greetings
Haere Mai! • Welcome!
Haere ra • Goodbye
Kapai • Good
Aue! • Alas!

INDEX

Note: Numbers in **bold** indicate photographs